# seven

# seven

### A MODERN DAY
### LOOK AT THE FEASTS
### OF THE LORD

TRICIA JOHNSON

MISTY DOLLARD

Ignite Worldwide Ministries

# Contents

# God's Appointed Times

The Lord said to Moses, "These are my appointed [feasts], the appointed [feasts] of the LORD, which you are to proclaim as sacred assemblies" (Leviticus 23:2). The Feasts of the Lord (or in some Bible translations, the Festivals of the Lord), when looked at both individually and as a whole, paint a beautiful picture of God's redemptive plan for man. Before God spoke light into existence, before He breathed life into Adam, God knew. He knew man would fall into the grip of sin and would need to be restored, redeemed, and made new. The Lord knew a sacrifice would be required, a Savior needed. Redemption is at the core of who God is, and throughout the pages of Scripture we see Him telling the story of man's redemption in various ways. But there is one place where we find the complete story of redemption laid out for all humankind, from beginning to end: the appointed Feasts of the Lord.

God appointed seven feasts. Four take place in the spring and three take place in the fall. The four spring feasts are Passover, the Feast of Unleavened Bread, the Feast of Firstfruits, and the Feast of Weeks. The three fall feasts are the Feast of Trumpets, the Day of Atonement, and the Feast of Tabernacles. All seven of the Lord's feasts join perfectly to show us His redemptive plan fulfilled through Jesus, our Messiah.

It is our belief that, while the feasts were designated for the Jewish community, we as Gentile believers have received not only an inheritance through Jesus but also a heritage. We believe the Feasts of the Lord are a part of every believer's heritage, given to us through the blood of the Lamb. Just as salvation is for Jew and Gentile alike, so too are the blessings associated with the feasts. Because of the work accomplished on the cross by Jesus, the Son of God, Gentiles have been grafted into the Hebraic root of Abraham. While Gentiles are not required to keep the feasts, knowledge of them enhances our faith as we understand more about our Savior. They are an exciting, living inheritance all believers in Christ Jesus can receive because, as you will learn, not only did our Savior celebrate the feasts, but He also fulfilled them.

The feasts are a time for believers to come together in acts of remembrance and giving thanks; they are consecrated times for atonement of sins and special times to ask for blessings. God intended every feast as a time to draw near to the Lord and be with Him. No matter how far from God their paths took them, seven times a year the Lord offered opportunity for His people to meet with Him for holy purposes, to ensure sin would not keep them from Him.

In the Bible the number seven—which occurs over and over in the feasts and in all of Scripture, from Genesis to Revelation, from creation to the end—means "perfection; completion." It comes from a Hebrew word meaning "to be full; to have enough; to be satisfied." On the seventh day God rested from His perfect creative work designing our world. Seven days after the Israelites began their march around the walls of Jericho, seven trumpets sounded seven times and the walls came tumbling down. Naaman the leper washed seven times in the Jordan and was cleansed. John's Revelation addresses seven churches and speaks of seven seals, seven trumpets being sounded, and seven bowls being poured out as the Final Days are completed and satisfied. And God ordained seven feasts, each satisfying a part of God's redemptive plan.

The first feast is Passover. It is the foundational feast upon which all the other feasts build and rest. But before we begin we must have an understanding of Jewish days.

## JEWISH DAYS

The Jewish day begins in the evening at sundown and continues through the daylight hours until the following sundown. Sundown to sundown, or evening to evening, is considered one day. The celebration of Jewish holidays always begins at sundown—when the day has technically begun. The seven days in a Hebrew week are simply referred to as "the first day," "the second day," "the third day," and so forth. The seventh day, however, is unique because it is set apart from the others and given a special name: the "Sabbath." It is a day of rest and worship. Keep these days and times in mind when studying the feasts as they will aid in your understanding of God's appointed times.

## A WORD ABOUT BIBLE TRANSLATION

We primarily use the New International Version of the Bible in this study, and the word *feast* has been replaced by *festival* in the latest NIV update (2011). Our preference, however, is *feast*, so we have elected to substitute *feast* for *festival* in brackets when we quote from the NIV.

As you begin this study, it is our prayer that you will find great joy in studying your heritage through the feasts. We hope you will be filled with enlightenment as you come away with a new understanding of the things of old. May your knowledge of God be enriched as you draw closer in heart and mind to the Lord.

*Tricia Johnson and Misty Dollard*

# CHAPTER 1

# Passover

PRAISE BE TO THE LORD, WHO RESCUED YOU FROM
THE HAND OF THE EGYPTIANS AND OF PHARAOH.

EXODUS 18:10

In the desert lands of Egypt, we find the Israelites. It's been more than four hundred years since the ancestors of Jacob arrived, looking for refuge and a new place to call home. Once welcomed by the rulers of the land, now the Israelites are slaves under a heavy and brutal hand. Abused and neglected, they feel forgotten and abandoned by the God of their fathers— the God of Abraham, Isaac, and Jacob.

For generations God's chosen people had grown in numbers and strength, leading to the ruling king's feeling threatened and afraid. Pharaoh's answer was to oppress and enslave the Hebrews, making their lives as hopeless and painful as possible. Freedom from this oppression was nothing more than a distant thought for the Israelites, a fleeting hope of rescue from the miry clay that surrounded and defined their hard-pressed lives. Four hundred years, and then God spoke to a man named Moses.

# seven

The Lord said, "I have indeed seen the misery of my people in Egypt. I have heard them crying out because of their slave drivers, and I am concerned about their suffering. So I have come down to rescue them from the hand of the Egyptians and to bring them up out of that land into a good and spacious land, a land flowing with milk and honey." (Exodus 3:7–8)

The Lord summoned Moses, telling him the Great I AM was going to move on behalf of His people. Moses appeared before Pharaoh, speaking these words as instructed by the Lord: "Let my people go, so that they may worship me" (Exodus 7:16). But Pharaoh's heart was hard and unyielding, his answer always no. Nine plagues were sent upon the land of Egypt and its inhabitants, but still the ruler's heart and mind could not be changed. The Nile River and all the water in Egypt turned to blood. The country was overrun with frogs; then came the gnats and flies. The livestock in the Egyptian fields died, and boils festered on the skin of all the Egyptian people. Still Pharaoh's heart remained hard. Next came an all-out assault on the land as hail fell from the sky and locusts devoured what little was left in their fields. Darkness overtook Egypt, and for three straight days the blackest sky was their reality—so dark no one dared leave their home except for the Israelites. God had provided them with light and protection.

Throughout the days and weeks of the nine plagues, God was sending a message to all who dared to listen. He was dealing with

Pharaoh and the hardness of his heart, but He was also g.
His chosen people the opportunity to watch their Lord in acti ...
God knew what the last and final plague would be, but He needed
to build the faith of His followers along the way before He asked
them to put their hope and trust in Him. He was providing them
with visible and tangible signs of His miraculous power, His
protection and favor, and most important, His love. It was as if
God was saying to them through His actions, "Trust in Me; trust
in Me." Through each of the plagues, God desired a faith in Him
to be created. He looked to instill in the Israelites a confidence
and trust that would move them from being a hopeless people
into a people of faith and action.

After the darkness came one last and final plague. This
plague was so colossal that the Lord needed to prepare Moses
in advance for what was to come. Read Exodus 11:1–8. What
did God say would be the tenth and final plague?

The tenth and final plague, the plague of the firstborn, is
now known as Passover (*Pesach*). Passover was an actual event
that happened only once. It so radically shaped the history of the
Israelite people that the Lord commanded it to be remembered
and celebrated every year. But Passover is not just about histc
nor just about death. The real story is about life.

# seven

God said He would make a distinction between Egypt and Israel, but that distinction would come at a price. Read Exodus 12:1–14 and answer the questions below.

Who was Moses to tell of God's instructions?

On what day were the Israelites instructed to take a lamb into their home?

What kind of lamb was it to be?

What were they instructed to do with the lambs for four days?

What were they to do with the lambs on the fourteenth day?

First, God says "tell the whole community" (v. 3). Tell the whole community what? Tell them on the tenth day they are to bring a lamb into their homes and care for it until the fourteenth day, when all the people of the community will gather and slaughter the lambs at twilight (v. 6). The Hebrew nation had just witnessed God doing incredible things all around them. They were no longer to be merely observers but doers. Their role was no longer about watching God do all the work but about putting faith into action. Their first command was to find a lamb and take care of it. The Hebrew words used in the phrase "take care of" are *hāyāh*, meaning "to become," and *mišmeret*, meaning "responsible for what is cared for; to guard, to watch." God was instructing the families to bring unblemished lambs into their homes and care for them as if they were a part of the family. Four days was just enough time to become attached to the animal, to bond with it. God wanted to ensure those feelings of attachment.

You see, the people needed to understand that the sacrifice that would save them would cost the life of one who was spotless and blameless. God wanted to ensure they grasped that an innocent one would die in their place.

With the plague quickly approaching, the Israelite community gathered together to publicly sacrifice the Passover lambs that would redeem them from the coming judgment. Once the instructions of the sacrifice had been carried out, what were the next steps the Israelites were to follow, as spoken in Exodus 12:7–11?

They were to take the blood and place it on the tops and sides of the doorframes of their homes. When the judgment of death passed through the land of Egypt, the blood would serve as a sign of all who chose to believe—a symbol of distinction. Write out Exodus 12:13.

"When I see the blood, I will pass over you." Here we can already see God teaching His people the significance of the power of the blood. The blood on the doorpost was a symbol of belief to the Lord, a symbol of one's faith in Him. The Lord spoke to Moses, Moses spoke to the people, and the people acted in obedience. The Bible tells us the Lord struck down all the firstborn males in Egypt at midnight, from the firstborn of Pharaoh to the firstborn of the prisoner and even the firstborn of all the livestock. Those with the blood displayed on their homes, however, were saved from death. Why? The blood of the sacrificial lamb was powerful enough to save lives. It was powerful enough to cause death to have no effect on them and powerful enough for the destroyer to be rendered helpless at the sight of it. Throughout Scripture we see sins can be forgiven only by the shedding of blood. The purpose of a blood sacrifice is to cover, cleanse, and deliver us from sin. Therefore the blood must be from a source without defect. Without the shedding of blood there is no forgiveness (Hebrews 9:22).

We have read the instructions God gave regarding the event of Passover. Pick up the story in Exodus 12:29–42. How did the night of Passover conclude?

Our world has seen its fair share of overwhelming devastation from war across its lands. But on that night there was no war, no battle. Not even a fight commenced. Except for those who, by faith, spread the Passover blood on their homes, not one person in all of Egypt was unaffected. Can you imagine the sound of an entire nation wailing across a land where death ensued all at once? Most of us reading these words have tasted the sting of death and the pain that accompanies such loss. Put that on a national level and it becomes unimaginable. Yet even among such widespread death, there was still life—the lives of those who acted in obedience and faith, who covered themselves with the blood.

The mighty Pharaoh, worshiped as a god, had been dealt a judgment not even his princely throne could escape. Moses and Aaron were summoned to the throne and instructed to take the people out of the land of Egypt. The entire nation of Israel—

men and women, young and old, flocks and herds—began their journey to a place God had prepared for them. A place where they would be free to worship their Lord, a place filled with milk and honey, a place of fellowship and prosperity.

## FIRSTS

With the story of Passover, we witness God's redeeming love offered through the sacrifice of a lamb, but there is one more important detail to examine before we close this lesson. Go back and read Exodus 12:1–2. Prior to God's telling Moses and Aaron how to prepare for the coming Passover, what was the very clear message He shared with them?

Before the Israelites ever left Egypt, God was ordaining for them a new way of life, a new beginning. Their old way of life—one of slavery, bondage, and hardship—was going to be replaced by a life of freedom, a life full of new beginnings and second chances. God wanted to solidify this to them. He yearned for His chosen ones to know that with salvation comes newness, with redemption comes freedom, and with faith a new walk begins. "This month is to be for you the first the first month of your year" (Exodus 12:2). While Go of the "first month" twice, He used two different Hebrew words. The "first" used at the beginning of the sentence is the word *rōš* and it means "chief, top, leader." The month of Nisan (as it is called today) was to be the top month for the nation of Israel, the leader of all the rest of the months, their chief month. It was as if God was saying to them, "Right here, right now, we are establishing a new way of doing things."

TODAY—becomes the first day of your new life with Me.
TODAY—is the first day of the rest of your months.

This is a concept Paul conveyed in his letters to the believers in Corinth when he told them the old has gone and the new has come (2 Corinthians 5:17).

The second "first" is the word *rišôn*, meaning "foremost (of position), former, beginning (of time)." God was establishing a new way of keeping track of their time, their years, their new life.

TODAY—will be your leader.
THIS MONTH—is to be for you the leader of all the rest.

God knew His people would need not just a change of scenery and a new leader but an entirely new life, a new identity. A new life marked by a specific new beginning. A beginning they could then remember and celebrate as holy from that day forward, generation after generation.

When we think of new beginnings, we are reminded of Isaiah 43:18–19. Record those verses in the space below.

The Message words these particular verses so beautifully. It says, "Forget about what's happened; don't keep going over old history. Be alert, be present. I'm about to do something brand-new. It's bursting out! Don't you see it? There it is! I'm making a road through the desert, rivers in the badlands."

It's as if those thoughts were already formed in God's mind when He said, "This is to be the first month of your year." As if He was saying, "Be alert, my chosen ones, because I am about to blow the dirt off your mud-stained tunics. My beloved people, your new life deserves a new calendar, so don't look back; don't focus on what was. Keep your eyes focused on what I am about to do from here on out."

# JESUS IN PASSOVER

*Yeshua (Salvation)* in Passover

In every aspect of Passover we see a foreshadowing of Christ. God in His infinite wisdom established a perfect plan for the Israelites to escape their slave masters, to escape death, as well as a way to remember all He had done for them for generations to come. Within that perfect plan we see God establishing The Perfect Plan. The Son, the Lamb of God, would be given as a way for all peoples of all nations to escape death, to escape their slave masters and walk into their Promised Land. Let's take an in-depth look at Passover and the symbolism shared with Christ.

## JESUS, THE LAMB OF GOD

"Christ, our Passover Lamb, has been sacrificed."
(1 Corinthians 5:7)

Jesus lived a perfect and sinless life, qualifying Him to be our one and only Passover Lamb. As the Lamb of God, He was the unblemished sacrifice that took the burden of our sin, removed it, and made us holy before a Holy God. The blood of a perfect lamb was required for the salvation of the Israelites, and the blood of the Perfect Lamb was required for the salvation of the world. Read John 1:29. What does John the Baptist say about Jesus?

Check which term Paul uses to refer to Christ in 1 Corinthians 5:7.

- ☐ Our Redeemer
- ☐ Our Savior
- ☐ Our Passover Lamb

According to 1 Peter 1:18–19, how were we redeemed?

In the last book of the Bible, we read about the revelation of Christ, given to John, about what must soon take place (Revelation 1:1). In the fifth chapter of Revelation, the Lamb is revealed. Read the entire chapter, writing down all the details you find about the Lamb.

"Then I saw a Lamb, looking as if it had been slain" (v. 6).
"Worthy is the Lamb, who was slain" (v. 12). Jesus, the Lamb of
God, was slain, and with His blood we have been purchased,
redeemed, and saved from eternal death, which passes over us.
Isaiah speaks boldly of this truth in Isaiah 53. Read through the
entire chapter, making note of all the descriptions of the One
whom Isaiah is foretelling.

Of whom is the prophet foretelling?

Write out verse 7 (notice the numbering of this key verse
regarding our Savior).

Circle all the words or phrases below describing who is sacrificed, as found in verses 8–12.

Many descendants    No deceit in mouth    Guilt offering

Bear iniquities of many    Lamb of God    Made intercession

Jesus, the One God declared in Matthew 3:17 ("This is my Son, whom I love"), is the true Passover Lamb. He is the Lamb who laid down His life to take away the sins of the world. The Lamb in whose blood are strength, power, and freedom.

# BETHLEHEM

Every lamb used in the sacrifices performed at the temple, including those for Passover, was born and raised in Bethlehem on the hills above Jerusalem. The *Migdal Eder*, otherwise known as the Tower of the Flock, was the place on the hillsides surrounding Bethlehem where lambs destined for the temple sacrifices would be found. Every firstborn male lamb was considered to be holy and was set aside to be given as a sacrifice in Jerusalem.

Read Luke 2:1–7. Check the place where was Jesus born.

☐ Nazareth        ☐ Judea

☐ Capernaum       ☐ Bethlehem

John 7:42 says, "Does not Scripture say that the Messiah will come from David's descendants and from Bethlehem, the town where David lived?" You see, those of the Jewish faith believed

Christ would come from David's family. They leaned on the prophecy of Micah, which tells of Israel's coming King. Write down the words of Micah 5:2.

Just as the lambs sacrificed for the Passover celebration came from the hills above Jerusalem, so too did our Passover Lamb. The small, insignificant town called Bethlehem birthed the most significant Lamb ever to walk the face of the earth.

## A WEEK IN THE LIFE OF THE LAMB

"Take care of them until the fourteenth day of the month."
(Exodus 12:6)

Recall from earlier, what do the words "take care of" mean in the original Hebrew language?

According to Exodus 12:3, on what day was the lam
taken into the home?

On the tenth day of the month of Nisan, the Passover lambs
were herded down the hills of Bethlehem into the sprawling
city of Jerusalem. Families gathered around the herd of bleating
lambs, pointing and discussing which lamb to bring into their
home. Nurturing and guarding the precious animals would have
already begun. On that very day, Christ made His triumphal
entry into the Holy City. Jesus, the Passover Lamb, was being
welcomed "home" into Jerusalem. Shouts of "Hosanna" rose
into the air. "Save now, save now," the people were saying. Our
Lamb, save us. For the next four days the Lamb of God would
be found teaching in the temple. He would be in His Father's
house, where day after day people would come to hear Him as
He nurtured others with His words (Luke 21:37–38).

The triumphal entry of Jesus into Jerusalem is recorded in all
four of the Gospels. Upon reading through the printed Scriptures,
underline or highlight the following information:

1. Who gathered to welcome Jesus?
2. What were the actions of the people gathered?
3. What was announced as Jesus was entering Jerusalem?

# seven

*Matthew 21:6–11*

The disciples went and did as Jesus had instructed them. They brought the donkey and the colt and placed their cloaks on them for Jesus to sit on. A very large crowd spread their cloaks on the road, while others cut branches from the trees and spread them on the road. The crowds that went ahead of him and those that followed shouted, "Hosanna to the Son of David!" "Blessed is he who comes in the name of the Lord!" "Hosanna in the highest heaven!" When Jesus entered Jerusalem, the whole city was stirred and asked, "Who is this?" The crowds answered, "This is Jesus, the prophet from Nazareth in Galilee."

*Mark 11:1–11*

As they approached Jerusalem and came to Bethphage and Bethany at the Mount of Olives, Jesus sent two of his disciples, saying to them, "Go to the village ahead of you, and just as you enter it, you will find a colt tied there, which no one has ever ridden. Untie it and bring it here. If anyone asks you, 'Why are you doing this?' say, 'The Lord needs it and will send it back here shortly.' They went and found a colt outside in the street, tied at a doorway. As they untied it, some people standing there asked, "What are you doing untying that colt?" They answered as Jesus had told them to, and the people let them go. When they brought the colt to Jesus and threw their cloaks over it, he sat on it. Many people spread their cloaks on the road, while others spread branches they had cut in the fields. Those who went ahead and those who followed shouted, "Hosanna!"

"Blessed is he who comes in the name of the Lord!" "Blessed is the coming kingdom of our father David!" "Hosanna in the highest heaven!" Jesus entered Jerusalem and went into the temple courts. He looked around at everything, but since it was already late, he went out to Bethany with the Twelve.

*Luke 19:37–40*

When he came near the place where the road goes down the Mount of Olives, the whole crowd of disciples began joyfully to praise God in loud voices for all the miracles they had seen: "Blessed is the king who comes in the name of the Lord!" "Peace in heaven and glory in the highest!" Some of the Pharisees in the crowd said to Jesus, "Teacher, rebuke your disciples!" "I tell you," he replied, "if they keep quiet, the stones will cry out."

*John 12:12–15*

The next day the great crowd that had come for the [feast] heard that Jesus was on his way to Jerusalem. They took palm branches and went out to meet him, shouting, "Hosanna!" "Blessed is he who comes in the name of the Lord!" "Blessed is the king of Israel!" Jesus found a young donkey and sat on it, as it is written: "Do not be afraid, Daughter Zion; see, your king is coming, seated on a donkey's colt."

Can you envision the throngs of people gathered along the roadside descending down the Mount of Olives? A great crowd carefully placed themselves along a steep dirt road, each one pressing in to get just a little bit closer to the One who was coming in the name of the Lord. Scores of people joyfully praised God as they spread their cloaks and branches along the path as a sign of reverence and adoration to the Son of God.

Jesus, the true Passover Lamb, was welcomed into His "home" of Jerusalem just a few days before His life would be sacrificed. Just as God called the whole community to gather and take the lambs into their homes, the community gathered to bring Jesus into His final earthly home as well.

## RIDDING THE LEAVEN

After Jesus' triumphal entry into Jerusalem, He immediately went straight to His Father's house. Mark 11:11 tells us, "Jesus entered Jerusalem and went into the temple courts. He looked around at everything, but since it was already late, he went out to Bethany with the Twelve." Not only was Jesus welcomed "home" as He entered Jerusalem, He was also going "home" to the temple. Jesus wanted to be with the presence of the Lord. The Son was going back to the Father's house; He was going home.

The temple courts were where Jesus was found for the remainder of the days prior to His death. The day after arriving in Jerusalem, we see Jesus head to the temple courts a second here He proceeds to rid the leaven.

Read Mark 11:15–18 and Luke 19:45–48. What did Jesus do upon entering the temple courts?

Picture the scene you just read about. Jesus is standing in the house of the Lord, and everywhere He looks He sees people bringing disgrace upon the holy grounds of His courtyards. People wander from booth to booth, searching for the perfect gift to give the Lord. The aroma of food being cooked and the strong stench of animals consume every sense of smell the body has. Ears try to tune out the clamor of haggling vendors, laughing children, and bleating sheep in every direction. People everywhere look either for a bargain or to make a profit. Jesus says His home has been turned into a den of robbers. This house of prayer has become anything but that, and to the Son of God, this is sinful. The temple is being desecrated. And so He will "drive out" all who are participating in this sinful act.

What we must understand is that certain rituals and restrictions surrounding the celebration of Passover and the sacrifice of the Passover lamb were required by God. Ridding the home of leaven (representing impurities or sin) was one of those rituals. For instance, Exodus 12:14–15 is where we find

God's instructions regarding yeast and the home. What does it say the people are to do?

A ceremony called *Bedikat Hamez* is performed at Passover; it means "searching for leaven." This ceremony of cleansing one's home involves going to great lengths to search for even the smallest particle of *hamez* (leaven) and then ridding it from the home. This is a requirement for the celebration of Passover. We see Jesus doing just that, cleansing His home of leaven by driving out those buying and selling in the temple courts.

## INSPECTION

We have learned that just as the Passover lambs came from Bethlehem, so too did Jesus. The lambs were taken into the homes on the tenth day of the month of Nisan, the same day Jesus traveled the road from Bethany home to Jerusalem. In preparation for the Passover celebration and the Feast of Unleavened Bread, all homes were to be cleansed of leaven and made pure. Jesus ensured the leaven was removed from His home by driving out the money changers from the temple courts. As we continue to travel down the road to Calvary, we see another similarity between Messiah and the Passover lambs: inspection.

In the days leading up to Jesus' death, He remained at the temple, doing what He had previously done: preaching, teaching, and healing. The chief priests and teachers of the law questioned and challenged Him, inspecting Christ the Passover Lamb thoroughly. They questioned His authority and, according to Luke 22:2, they did everything they could to "get rid of Jesus."

Describe the scene in Matthew 21:23–27, 45–46; 22:15.

According to Luke 20:20–26, were the teachers and chief priests successful in trapping Jesus in His own words?

For years the Pharisees and Sadducees had been trying to find a way to ensnare Jesus with His own words as they sought ways to kill Him. Their actions this week leading up to Passover were nothing new. They were examining Jesus, inspecting Him. The religious leaders were doing all they could to find fault with

Him, to find Him marked in some way: imperfect, blemished, or spotted.

Every Passover lamb had to be thoroughly examined, a process by which the priests confirmed that the lambs were fit to be considered a holy sacrifice. Because God required a lamb without defects, each lamb was carefully scrutinized before its acceptance. Testing the Lamb of God with a barrage of questions implied this was all part of the custom of Passover. A blemish, a spot, something imperfect about Him would mean the priests could disqualify Jesus as Messiah.

The examination that began the day after Jesus entered Jerusalem continued right up to the hours immediately preceding His death. According to John 18:12–13, where was Jesus taken after He was arrested?

Mark 14:53–65 tells us what happened once Jesus was taken to the high priest. Read the Scripture slowly and with great thought, paying close attention to words such as *evidence, testimony, condemned,* and *accused.*

As Jesus stood before the council of those looking to kill Him, He was once again interrogated. When asked if He was the Christ, His answer was a simple "I am." In the eyes of those investigating Jesus, this was all they needed to find fault in Him. Finally the blemish they had been searching for flowed from the lips of the truly unblemished. In their minds a spot had appeared. A spot to which they could point and say, "This man is not Messiah, for He has spoken blasphemy against God." They hauled Him away to the ruling Romans, where He would be "examined" once again. Read Luke 23:1–15. Who questioned Jesus?

What were Pilate's words to the Israelites gathered outside the palace according to Luke 23:14–15?

From the time Jesus entered through the gates of the temple and throughout the four days leading to His arrest, the religious leaders of the nation of Israel were bent on their inspection of the Lamb of God. This inspection continued all the way up to His death sentencing. The intense scrutiny, the ever-so-crafty questions, the never-ending observation all focused on one lamb, the Lamb of God—the One who came to redeem from death every man from every nation, tribe, and tongue.

seven

## PUBLIC DISPLAY

According to Mark's gospel account (15:1), it was very early in the morning when the chief priests bound Jesus and brought Him before Pilate. The chief priests, elders, and teachers of the law finally had what they needed to condemn Him to death. In the beginning hours of daylight, Jesus was interrogated by Pilate and then by Herod, after which He was flogged, beaten, and ultimately sentenced to death. Jesus was led to the Place of the Skull, otherwise known as Golgotha. There, on the top of a hill, He was brutally nailed to a cross and raised up for all to see. The Lamb of God was put on public display. Read and record how the public was involved with Jesus' death according to Mark 15:21–32.

On the morning of the fourteenth day of the month of Nisan, the Passover lamb was to be bound on the altar in the temple courts for the entire community to see. On public display, the sacrifice was to be witnessed by all who gathered there. So too was our Passover Lamb put on display. His body was bound to His altar and sacrificed for those who gathered to witness the scene. His pain and suffering were evident to all who looked upon His tortured body, just as Isaiah prophesied.

Just as there were many who were appalled at him—his
appearance was so disfigured beyond that of any human being
and his form marred beyond human likeness. (Isaiah 52:14)

Not only was the Lamb of God put on public display, but the
timing of His display was neither accidental nor coincidental.
Rather it was all a perfectly timed display of how detailed our
God was to prove beyond a shadow of a doubt that the Son of
God is the true Passover Lamb.

Read Mark 15:25, 33–34; Luke 23:44–45; and Matthew
27:45–46, then fill in the columns below accordingly.

| Time of Day | What Happened |
| --- | --- |
|  |  |

The "third hour" does not mean it was three o'clock in the
morning. According to Jewish law, an hour is calculated by
taking the time from sunrise to sunset and dividing it into 12
equal parts. Therefore, the third hour, when Jesus was crucified,
was approximately 9:00 a.m. on Friday morning. This was also
the time when the lambs were to be bound on the altar. The
same time the Passover lambs were being bound in the temple

31

courts, so too were the nails being driven through Jesus' wrists and feet. As the lamb lay tied to the sacred place for all to see, Jesus hung from a tree, visible to all who turned their gaze toward the top of the hill.

At high noon, or the sixth hour, the sun disappeared and darkness consumed the land. As the life was slowly and painfully being drained from Messiah's body, so too the life was being drained from the sky. At the ninth hour, after six grueling hours of hanging by only His wrists and feet, Jesus spoke His final words and succumbed to death. Record word for word what John 19:30 tells us Jesus spoke immediately before He died.

According to Jewish custom, at precisely three o'clock in the afternoon, or the ninth hour, the high priest would approach the lamb that was bound to the altar. The priest would cut its throat and declare to the community, "It is finished." The Greek word for "finished," used in John 19:30 is *teleo*, meaning "end; goal; to accomplish or fulfill; to complete or accomplish something, not merely by ending it, but bringing it to perfection or its destined goal."

The redemptive work of the true Passover Lamb had been completed. The sacrifice of the blood of the Lamb had been received unto the Lord, covering over every sin and granting salvation for all humankind. As believers we know death had no hold on Jesus, as He was raised from the dead and seated at the right hand of the Father. Jesus brought God's redemptive plan to its destined goal: salvation for all who put their faith in the blood of the Lamb.

We have looked in detail at what occurred in Jesus' life the week leading up to His death. We have seen how the Passover lambs and the Lamb of God were experiencing the very same things at the very same time. On the next page is a visual representation of the timeline to solidify these details in your mind.

Nisan:

|  | Sacrificial Passover Lamb | Jesus Our Passover Lamb |
|---|---|---|
| 10th | Entry into Jerusalem | Entry into Jerusalem |
| 11th | Inspection by the priests | Inspection by the priests |
| 12th | Inspection by the priests | Inspection by the priests |
| 13th | Inspection by the priests | Inspection by the priests |
| 14th | Public display and sacrifice | Public display and sacrifice |

(Jewish days begin at sundown and continue until the following sundown.)

Before God established Passover, He had already chosen the Lamb. Before the people established the customs and traditions of the Passover lambs, God had already fulfilled them all in His Son. Before the year of Christ's death came to be, the Lord's timeline of events was already written. Nothing was random, nothing was forgotten.

## PERSONAL APPLICATION

Has God ever asked you to take a step of faith, saying, "Trust in me"? Did you walk the path He asked or walk your own way? What was the outcome of your choice?

Jesus chose to be our redemption, granting salvation for all humankind. What does His sacrifice mean to you personally?

Just as no detail was left out of the life of Jesus, we can be confident that no detail will be left out of our lives. Take some time to think back through your life and pick one area where you can see God in the "details" (e.g., your gifting, your career, or your coming to Christ.). Write those details below.

# CHAPTER 2

# Passover Observance

While the actual event of Passover occurred only once, the celebration of this foundational feast has since become the longest continued celebration in history. The remembrance of Passover is what God ordained to be celebrated from generation to generation. God knew the powerful message of Passover and wanted to ensure that His people would not only remember what He had done for them but also understand the importance of the sacrifice. Begin by writing out Exodus 12:14.

To truly appreciate the importance God placed on this remembrance celebration, we need to look at the root meanings in the Hebrew language.

**Commemorate** (*Zikkaron*): a memorial, remembrance, record, account, celebration. This is an object reminder or token act by which something is brought to mind.

**Generations to come** (*Dor*): to encircle, surround. The duration of a person's life. Denotes the cycle of a person's lifetime, the time from the conception and birth of a person until the conception and birth of his or her offspring.

**Lasting** (*Olam*): without end; forever; perpetual, endless time; duration of time extended into the indefinite future; as long as one lives.

**Ordinance** (*Chuqqah*): decree; statute; law; custom. Denotes precepts and rules that must be strictly obeyed. Denotes an ordinance from God that was permanently binding.

In the Complete Jewish Bible, Exodus 12:14 reads as follows: "This will be a day for you to remember and celebrate as a festival to ADONAI; from generation to generation you are to celebrate it by a perpetual regulation."

God was telling His chosen people that Passover was to be a celebration, a memorial that occurred over the course of one's entire life, and this remembrance was to be an everlasting custom. The act of celebrating Passover was to be an object reminder to the people, an act by which the saving power of the blood of the lamb is brought to mind, an act to be kept from generation to generation as a lasting ordinance. The next two verses in Exodus 12 continue with God's specific instructions for the celebration of Passover. Read verses 15 and 16.

How many days were the Israelites not to eat yeast?

What were they to hold on the first and seventh day?

This assembly was a congregational meeting, a gathering of the people who had been consecrated to God. The congregation gathered before the Lord on the first day of Passover to remember that they had been declared sacred by a Holy God. The assemblies were for the people to remember who God had called them to be and to celebrate what God had done for them.

From the very beginning God gave specific instructions to Moses about the continued celebration of Passover. He again reiterates the importance of this event a few verses later, in Exodus 12:24–27 (printed below). Circle any references to celebrating the remembrance of Passover you find.

Obey these instructions as a lasting ordinance for you and your descendants. When you enter the land that the LORD will give you as he promised, observe this ceremony. And when your children ask you, "What does this ceremony mean to you?" then tell them, "It is the Passover sacrifice to the LORD, who passed over the houses of the Israelites in Egypt and spared our homes when he struck down the Egyptians."

The King James Version uses the word *service* in place of the word *ceremony*: "Ye shall keep this service." This is where we see God establishing the celebration of Passover as a service. The children would ask the parents, "What does this service mean to you?" In turn, God's children may have asked Him, "What does this service mean to you, Lord?" His answer is found in Leviticus 23:1–2: "And the Lord spoke to Moses, saying, 'Speak to the children of Israel and say to them: "The feasts of the Lord, which you shall proclaim to be holy convocations, these are My feasts"' (NKJV).

To truly appreciate God's answer, it is necessary to look again at the Hebrew root words and their meanings.

**Feasts** (*Moed*): an appointment, a fixed time, signal.

**Proclaim** (*Qara*): to call out, to proclaim, to pronounce; enunciating a specific message addressed to a specific recipient and intended to elicit a specific response.

**Convocation** (*Miqra*): something called out (e.g., a public meeting, a rehearsal).

Using the meanings of these words, God's answer would sound something like this: "The feasts I have declared are fixed times as well as signals used to proclaim and pronounce My rehearsals. My feasts are to be used to deliver a message to all who will perceive. They are the dress rehearsals for what is to come."

In His own words, God said the Israelites were to proclaim [the feasts] to be holy rehearsals. Why would He say that if He did not intend for there to be a "real performance?" One doesn't need a dress rehearsal if the real act is not going to follow. The remembrance of Passover served as a preparation for the performance of Jesus, the Lamb of God.

God was very specific as to how He wanted this service, this holy rehearsal, to look. His directives were simple and straightforward. To Moses, He said, "Celebrate this token act throughout the ages, from generation to generation. Include the most important things; the lamb, bitter herbs and unleavened bread, just as it was with the first Passover. Do this so the children will ask questions regarding the meaning of these customs" (Exodus 12:8, 14, 25, paraphrased). This brings us to the *Seder*, the Passover meal.

## SEDER

"That same night they are to eat the meat roasted over the fire, along with bitter herbs, and bread made without yeast." (Exodus 12:8)

Read Exodus 12:8–11. After they spread the blood on the doorframes of their homes, what were the Israelites to do?

According to Exodus 12:11, what is the name given to the meal eaten in haste?

The Lord's Passover is known as the *Seder* (pronounced SAY-der) and is derived from the Hebrew word meaning "order." While the exact origin of the Seder cannot be pinpointed, over time the celebration and its practices evolved into one that includes many rituals and customs. The Seder has a set order of events that includes Scripture readings, prayers, foods, songs, questions, and cups. Our focus in this observance section will be on four specific elements of the celebration. We will show how even from the beginning, God's lasting ordinance, which has been celebrated for close to 3,500 years, has always pointed to Messiah.

## THE PASSOVER LAMB

The first element is, most simply, the lamb. Read Exodus 12:8–9, 43, 46. What were the regulations God gave to Moses regarding the Passover lamb?

Notice the Passover lamb was not to have any of its bones broken, and the entire lamb, from head to foot, was to be roasted over the fire. Now read John 19:31–37. What is the messianic prophecy in verse 36?

Psalm 34:20 is the prophecy John was quoting. It says, "He protects all his bones, not one of them will be broken." From the very first lambs used during Passover to the prophecy-fulfilling Lamb of God, we see the support structure of the body remaining intact. Not one bone of the lambs sacrificed for Passover was to be broken, and as God would have it, not one of Christ's bones was broken through all the beatings, floggings, and nail-piercing torture He experienced.

# seven

The Passover lamb was to be roasted, cooked by fire. Yet it wasn't enough for the people to simply sacrifice the lamb; God also instructed them to partake of the lamb. The lamb wasn't to be merely looked upon; it was to be consumed. We believe this is a symbol of what we are to do with our Passover Lamb. Jesus does not want to be merely looked upon; He wants to be "consumed." Look at the recorded words of Jesus to see the symbolism so richly shown in Passover. Read John 6:50–51 and 57–58 below.

"Here is the bread that comes down from heaven, which anyone may eat and not die. I am the living bread that came down from heaven. Whoever eats this bread will live forever. This bread is my flesh, which I will give for the life of the world. . . . Just as the living Father sent me and I live because of the Father, so the one who feeds on me will live because of me. This is the bread that came down from heaven."

Jesus was speaking directly to the fact that He is to be consumed. Check all the statements below that apply to Jesus.

- ☐ He is the living bread.
- ☐ This bread is His flesh.
- ☐ He gave His life.

Fill in the blanks from Matthew 26:26:

"While they were eating, Jesus took bread, and when he had given thanks, he broke it and gave it to his disciples,

saying, 'Take and _____; this is
my _____.'"

Jesus wants to be consumed. He does not want to be purely a figure in our lives but desires to have an active role. Christ offers us life-giving sustenance, but we have to choose to partake. Speaking of Himself, He asked us to "take and eat," and we do that by allowing Him into our lives and walking with Him daily.

## MATZAH

The second element, the *matzah*, is unleavened bread (bread without yeast). The Seder service requires three pieces of matzah. Why three? In Jewish tradition there is no definitive answer, though previous rabbis have offered some explanations. One is that the three pieces of matzah represent the three different groups of Jewish people: the priests, Levites, and Israelites. A second tradition holds that the matzah represents the three patriarchs: Abraham, Isaac, and Jacob. For a believer in Christ, however, the symbolism is unmistakable. The three pieces of "sin-free" bread represent the Trinity of the Father, the Son, and the Holy Spirit—The Godhead, three in One.

In the first half of the Seder celebration, the matzah is important. Three pieces of unleavened bread, carefully wrapped in linen, are sitting on the table. Soon after the celebration begins, the middle piece is removed from the linen bag and broken in half. One half of the broken piece is returned to the linen bag

and the other half is wrapped in a linen napkin and hidden somewhere in the home. Once the food has been consumed, later in the service, the children search for the hidden piece and bring it back to the table. Everyone present takes a small piece to eat.

Jesus, the middle of the Godhead, came down from heaven and dwelled among His created people. He gave up Himself and died on a cross (broken), was buried (wrapped in linen and hidden away), and on the third day was resurrected (brought back).

The similarities between the matzah tradition and Jesus' sacrifice and resurrection don't end with the rituals of the

Passover ceremony. The process for making matzah requires the dough to be pierced. This is done to keep air from penetrating into the dough, giving it a flat, unrisen consistency. Upon baking, the holes create a striped effect on the unleavened bread, thereby causing it to have a striped and pierced appearance.

Read John 19:34. What happened to Jesus?

Write out the quotation in John 19:37.

Isaiah 53:5 says, "He was wounded for our transgressions, He was bruised for our iniquities; the chastisement for our peace was upon Him, and by His stripes we are healed" (NKJV).

Circle the words above that indicate the physical torment Christ suffered.

The body of Jesus Messiah was wounded and bruised— pierced and striped—for us, for our sins. It was through the act of piercing and His being striped that we become healed and whole.

## AFIKOMEN

The *afikomen* is the third specific element of the Seder meal on which we'll focus. Afikomen is a word given to the broken piece of matzah that is hidden and then found after the dinner is eaten. The afikomen was not a part of the Passover meal Jesus celebrated; it was added to the service at some point after His death. The word *afikomen* is a Greek word and first appeared in the Mishnah (the earliest collection of rabbinical rulings) around AD 200. For years Jewish rabbis have debated the meaning of this word because it does not exist in the Hebrew language. The agreement reached by leading rabbis is that afikomen means "dessert" since it follows the meal when dessert would usually be served.

However, as stated above, afikomen is a Greek word, derived from the Greek verb *ikneomai*, which means "I have come, I arrived, I came." So powerful, so simple. The middle matzah—broken, hidden, found, and then shared with all who are present—means "I came."

So how did a Greek word that seems to clearly point to Jesus become a part of this Jewish celebration? In AD 70, Rome ruled over Israel and destroyed the temple along with the city of Jerusalem. The Levitical law, by which the Hebrew nation lived, demanded that sacrifices be performed at the temple. No temple meant no sacrifice. No sacrifice meant no more Passover lambs. No Passover lambs meant the celebration and remembrance of Passover would now be threatened. To keep tradition alive, the afikomen replaced the lamb, becoming the symbol of the Passover sacrifice.

By this point in history many Jews did, however, believe in Jesus as Messiah. Read Acts 2:5 and 2:41 and fill in the blanks.

"Now there were staying in Jerusalem God-fearing Jews from every _____   _____ _____." "Those who accepted his message were baptized, and about _____ _____ were added to their number that day."

God-fearing Jews from as far away as one could imagine heard the message Peter spoke on the day of Pentecost, resulting in three thousand men believing in the good news of Christ. That number doesn't include the women and children who listened and believed, so we can assume the total number of believers was much higher. These newest believers of Messiah would have gone back to their towns, communities, and families, sharing the wonderful truth of what they had just learned.

By the time the temple was destroyed 40 years later, these Jewish believers already knew the Lamb had been sacrificed once and for all. The afikomen had taken its place in the Seder as a representation of the Passover Lamb who died for their salvation, and they were taking it as Christ commanded: "Do this in remembrance of me" (Luke 22:19). One can see how, throughout the ages, given the destruction of the temple, sacrifices being forbidden, and with the spread of the good news throughout the Jewish believers, the afikomen would take its rightful place among the Seder celebration.

## THE CUPS

Four cups of wine are used throughout the Seder service; one at the beginning, one in the middle, and two at the end. The number four was not randomly chosen. The four cups represent the four powerful statements spoken by the Lord to Moses when He promised to deliver the Israelite slaves, statements the Israelites are still remembering to this day.

Circle the four "I will" statements the Lord made to Moses.

"Say to the Israelites: 'I am the LORD, and I will bring you out from under the yoke of the Egyptians. I will free you from being slaves to them, and I will redeem you with an outstretched arm and with mighty acts of judgment. I will take you as my own people, and ... be your God.'" (Exodus 6:6–7)

Before the Almighty God acted, He stated His purposes to His people. He said, "This is what I am going to do for you—I am going to remove your yoke and set you apart. I am going to break your chains and then redeem you with an outstretched arm. I am not going to leave you; I am going to take you unto Myself, call you My own, and I will be your God." Each cup of the Passover celebration represents one of the four powerful statements God made. The Seder begins by pouring from the first cup, the Cup of Sanctification, and praying the "prayer of sanctification" (*Kiddush*):

Blessed are Thou, Adonai our God, King of the Universe, Who creates fruit of the vine. Blessed are You Lord, King of the Universe, who made us holy with His commandments and favored us, and gave us His holy Sabbath, in love and favor, to be our heritage, as a reminder of the Creation. It is the foremost day of the holy festivals marking the Exodus from Egypt. For out of all the nations You chose us and made us holy, and You gave us Your holy Sabbath, in love and favor, as our heritage. Blessed are You Lord, Who sanctifies the Sabbath.[1]

Prayers offered up to God, thanking Him for choosing and blessing His people, are at the forefront of the celebration of remembrance; thanking Him for setting them apart, because that is what "sanctification" means—to be set apart, to be made holy.

God said, "I will bring you out from under the yoke. You who were once separate from Me; you who have been enslaved; you who have carried much load; I am going to remove it all from you and set you apart for My use."

Not only did God sanctify the Israelites, who outwardly displayed their being set apart by spreading the lambs' blood, but Jesus, the Lamb of God, also sanctified us through His blood.

Write out Hebrews 13:12.

1 John J. Parsons, "Friday Night Kiddush," *hebrews4christian.com* (April 2015).

"For them I sanctify myself, that they too may be truly sanctified" (John 17:19).

Christ sanctified (set apart) Himself so we could be sanctified (set apart) and made holy before God. The Cup of Sanctification reminds the Israelites of their freedom from bondage, and for all believers it brings to memory the first act of our salvation plan set forth by God.

The second cup in the Seder is the Cup of Deliverance: "I will free you from being slaves." God accomplished this in a literal sense for the Israelites but also in a spiritual sense for all. Read David's words in Psalm 91:14–16. What does the Lord say He will do for those who love Him?

Freedom and deliverance from bondage is a theme Jesus communicated during His earthly ministry. In Luke 4:18–19 Jesus spoke of the prophecies of Isaiah concerning Messiah: "The Spirit of the Lord is on me, because he has anointed me to proclaim good news to the poor. He has sent me to proclaim freedom for the prisoners and recovery of sight for the blind, to set the oppressed free, to proclaim the year of the Lord's favor."

"To proclaim freedom for the prisoners and . . . set the oppressed free." In other words, the Anointed One will deliver

the captives and rescue those in chains. John 8:36 tells us, "If the Son sets you free, you will be free indeed." God knew we could not free ourselves from sin any more than the Israelites could free themselves from their slave masters. Therefore He sanctified His Son so we might be delivered. "He rescued us from the domain of darkness, and transferred us to the kingdom of His beloved Son, in whom we have redemption, the forgiveness of sins" (Colossians 1:13–14 NASB).

The third cup is the Cup of Redemption: "I will redeem you with an outstretched arm." It is one thing to have the heavy load removed from your shoulders; it is yet another to have the shackles that bind your ankles broken loose. One is not free until the ransom price has been paid. The word *redeem* means "to buy back something, someone, or something consecrated to God; to ransom; to release." First we see God removing the yoke, and then He breaks the chains. Next we see Him "buying back" what is His. The Lord first redeemed His chosen nation of Israel and then, through His Son, ransomed and redeemed the world.

Look up Matthew 20:28. What did the Son of Man come to do with His life?

Read Titus 2:14 regarding our Savior, Jesus Christ, and fill in the blanks.

"[Jesus Christ,] who _____ himself

for us to _____ us from all wickedness

and to _____ for himself a people that

are _____."

The Son of God paid our ransom with His own life. Our redemption price was set, one life for another, sinless for sinful, the Master for the slave. With His blood we were bought back.

The fourth and final cup of the Seder is the Cup of Acceptance. It represents the Lord's final statement, "I will take you as my own people and I will be your God." The desire of the Lord did not end with the Israelites' freedom from their Egyptian slave masters. Next, God called them His own, giving them a new identity. Through the work of Jesus, we have the same acceptance and promise. We have been redeemed and brought into the family of God.

> But when the set time had fully come, God sent his Son, born of a woman, born under the law, to redeem those under the law, that we might receive adoption to sonship. Because you are his sons, God sent the Spirit of his Son into our hearts, the Spirit who calls out, "Abba, Father." So you are no longer a slave, but God's child; and since you are his child, God has made you also an heir. (Galatians 4:4–7)

The fourth cup of wine immediately follows the third. There is nothing in between the two cups, just a natural flow one to the next. This should tell us something of how God works; there is nothing in between redemption and acceptance. One immediately follows the other, a natural flow from one to the next.

## THE LAST SUPPER

Understanding the four cups of Passover makes the next Scripture come alive with new energy. Look at Luke 22:19–20: "And he took bread, gave thanks and broke it, and gave it to them, saying, 'This is my body given for you; do this in remembrance of me.' In the same way, after the supper he took the cup, saying,

'This cup is the new covenant in my blood, which is poured out for you.'"

Within the body of Christ, we refer to this as the Lord's Supper, or communion. No matter what the title, the act is the same. Jesus used the matzah and the Cup of Redemption to institute His own remembrance. The Lamb of God redeemed the world through the spilling of His blood, and whenever the Cup of Redemption is poured, all that He accomplished and fulfilled is remembered.

After the meal had been eaten, the bread broken, and the wine poured, Jesus told His followers He would not drink the fourth cup, the Cup of Acceptance. Record the words of Messiah in Matthew 26:29.

Jesus was rejected, not accepted, by the Jewish leaders and teachers. While a few believed He was the Son of God, most Israelites did not. Jesus knew His acceptance by the Jewish nation would be a future acceptance, so we see our Savior patiently awaiting the fourth cup, waiting for those called His chosen people to accept and share in the last cup with Him.

## RECORDED PASSOVER OBSERVANCES

We have journeyed with Jesus into Jerusalem and studied His actions as He prepared for what would be His last feast on earth. We watched as the hands of God's clock were in perfect timing with that of the Passover celebration. We looked in detail at how Passover is remembered and how, in that remembrance, traces of Messiah are found everywhere. Now we will take a brief look at some of the recorded remembrances in Scripture, focusing on the events that surrounded their celebration.

## FIRST PASSOVER CELEBRATION

One year to the date of their exodus, the Israelites celebrated Passover in the desert, as instructed by the Lord. Below, circle any references to dates or times you find and underline what the Israelites did.

The LORD spoke to Moses in the Desert of Sinai in the first month of the second year after they came out of Egypt. He said, "Have the Israelites celebrate the Passover at the appointed time. Celebrate it at the appointed time, at twilight on the fourteenth day of this month, in accordance with all its rules and regulations." . . . The Israelites did everything just as the LORD commanded Moses. (Numbers 9:1–3, 5)

One year after the Lord passed over the land of Egypt and spared those who believed in the power of the blood, we see the Israelites doing everything the Lord asked of them. What had they been doing up to this point? God's chosen people had been starting a new life, with new guidelines, new practices, and new customs. In Leviticus we find God establishing His rules, His regulations, and His laws. In the first eight chapters of Numbers, a census is taken and the 12 tribes are arranged in camps. The tabernacle was set up and offerings brought to the Lord from each tribe. Everything seemed to be set in order. The nation of Israel was ready for their new life. God established His way for them and, in His perfect timing, concluded it, all right before they were to celebrate their first feast to the Lord.

## JOSHUA AND THE PEOPLE

Scripture does not record another Passover celebration until 39 years later, when another significant transition took place in the lives of the nation of Israel. Let's pick up the story in the book of Joshua.

Read Joshua 3:14–17. Circle below what had just occurred.

Crossed over the Jordan

Exited Egypt

Moses died

In Joshua 5:2–12 we read about what happened immediately after they crossed the Jordan. Give a description of the events that followed.

Here we find the Israelites, who had spent 40 years wandering all over the barren desert, waiting. Waiting for the Lord to say, "Welcome to your Promised Land." Then one day He swings the gate open wide and has them step forth into that land. But before they take too many steps forward, He must first be remembered. God's saving grace, His endless love, and the power of the blood must be remembered once again. Their sights were set on conquering Jericho, but before they could look around, they needed to look up. According to Joshua 4:19, what day did the Israelites cross over the Jordan?

"The tenth day of the first month." God was saying, "This day is to be for your new beginning, the first day of your new life in the land I promised you. First, consecrate yourselves through circumcision, the outward display of your being set apart to a Holy God. Then, come, let us celebrate together."

Notice the Israelites were being brought home into the land of the Shepherd on the very day the Passover lamb was brought into the homes 40 years before. Four days later, the celebration of a new beginning commences. God was restoring Passover to a nation that would need to see and experience His miraculous power. Battles lay ahead of them. Obstacles would surround them. Challenges would seem insurmountable. Yet the power of the blood of the Lamb was with them. God solidified that message to His people through the act of Passover. He was once again asking them to choose for themselves if they were going to live by faith or by sight.

## KING JOSIAH

As one continues through the pages of the Old Testament to the book of 2 Kings, the nation of Israel is found in a state of existence contrary to God's desire and plan for them. Year after year, Israel had been turning away from what was right in the eyes of the Lord, following the detestable practices of the people and nations around them. Altars to Baal were erected, sorcery and divination were practiced, and child sacrifices were made. Asherah poles and male shrine prostitutes littered Solomon's temple. Evil dominated Judah's kings and its culture. In fact, 2 Kings 21:9 says, "They did more evil than the nations the LORD had destroyed before the Israelites."

It is inconceivable to think a nation so full of corruption and evil could ever be brought back into right standing with a

Holy God. But that is exactly what happened. Second Kings 22 and 23 tell us of King Josiah's legacy, and we find mention of Passover once again.

When King Josiah was 26 years old, the book of the law (the Torah or divine law) was read before him. As the words of the Lord filled his ears, he tore his kingly robes and humbly wept in great mourning over what he had just heard. Josiah's response to the book of the law was to gather the people together, renew the covenant in the presence of the Lord, and reestablish Passover.

> The king stood by the pillar and renewed the covenant in the presence of the LORD—to follow the LORD and keep his commands, statutes and decrees with all his heart and all his soul, thus confirming the words of the covenant written in this book. Then all the people pledged themselves to the covenant. (2 Kings 23:3)

What was the response of the people found at the end of verse 3?

Josiah then went to work ridding the temple and the land of Judah of the "leaven" that had infiltrated it. Before Passover could be celebrated, the sin had to be removed. Josiah was sweeping through the land with a God-sized broom and brushing away all that had been infected by the "yeast." Then, to follow, he ordered a celebration of redemption and sanctification, saying, "Celebrate the Passover to the LORD your God, as it is written in this Book of the Covenant" (v. 21). Not since the days of the judges who led Israel, nor throughout the days of the kings of Israel and the kings of Judah, had any such Passover been observed.

The people had chosen to reestablish themselves with their God. A spiritual as well as literal cleansing had taken place, and the Israelites were ready to show their renewed faith in the Lord by observing Passover. They were ready to once again remember the greatness of their God and celebrate with reckless abandon. The foundational Feast of Passover was a symbol of the new beginning awaiting them. A new way of doing life lay before them, and this remembrance celebration was their way of declaring they were ready to walk down that road.

## EZRA

Next we come to a book written by a priest named Ezra, where we find the story of the Jewish exiles returning to Jerusalem from Babylon. In chapter 6 we see King Darius (king of Persia) issuing a decree for the diligent rebuilding of the temple in Jerusalem. The restoration of the second temple was completed almost 70 years after it had been destroyed and three years after the restoration work had begun. What does Ezra 6:16–22 say happened a little over a month after the temple was complete?

Once again in the history of the Hebrew people, God brings His people out of captivity into a land of freedom, and in His perfect timing, Passover just so happened to occur following the dedication of the newly rebuilt temple. What better way to show their love for the Lord than to celebrate the feast that started it all? Notice in Ezra 6:21 that the priest shares a valuable piece of information so easy to skim over. With whom did the exiled Jews eat the Passover?

The Israelites openly accepted anyone who chose to remove the pagan practices of their lives and follow after the One True God. This acceptance also extended to Gentiles who converted to Judaism. "The Israelites . . . [ate together] with all who had separated themselves from the unclean practices of their Gentile neighbors in order to seek the LORD" (Ezra 6:21). Why is this important? God shows us here that anyone who has accepted Him, anyone who has a personal faith in Him and is willing to separate him- or herself from the practices of the world, is able and accepted to partake in Passover. One does not need to be Jewish by blood; one only needs to have the faith in Him God desires.

Passover is not only for the Jews to celebrate but for all believers to celebrate. God instituted this feast as a remembrance, a memorial to the Lord. As believers in the true Passover Lamb, we celebrate Jesus through Passover. The God of Abraham, Isaac, and Jacob, the God who made a covenant with Abraham saying all nations would be blessed through him, that very same God ordained Passover to be a lasting ordinance for Abraham's descendants—all of them.

The question for us today is this: if Passover is for all of Abraham's descendants, both by blood and by being grafted in, why is the celebration of Passover not a part of church today? Though we can see how history has shaped many of the practices of the church today, some things will forever remain a mystery. One thing we must always remember, however, is that we have an enemy who "masquerades as an angel of light," and that enemy, Satan, "comes only to steal and kill and destroy" (2 Corinthians 11:14; John 10:10). You see, even Satan knows there is power in the story of Passover, power in the blood of the Lamb. Through prompting the actions of men throughout history, he has diligently worked to eradicate anything that may point people to this truth. Take for example the Roman emperor

Constantine the Great. In AD 325 he declared in the writing the Council of Nicea that Christians were to have "nothing in common with the Jews" and pronounced that Easter would now replace the celebration of Passover. Easter, the new celebration of the sacrifice of Jesus' life, would coincide with the celebration of the Roman goddess of spring, Ishtar or Eastre.

A few years later Constantine made yet another edict into law. The Council of Antioch, written in AD 345, declares, "If any bishop, presbyter or deacon will dare, after this decree, to celebrate Passover, the council judges them to be anathema from the Church. This council not only deposes them from ministry, but also any others who dare to communicate with them." The word *anathema* means "cursed." This means the leaders of the Christian church pronounced a curse on anyone who would dare to celebrate Passover.

These declarations against the church's celebrating any Jewish festival continued for another three hundred years through edicts written by church leaders. Armies were even sent through the empire, enforcing the prohibition of Passover on those who professed to be Christians. Why? Because Satan knows if he can steal Passover, he can steal the meaning of the message: there is power in the blood of the Lamb. Our enemy understands what Jesus did on the cross. He knows the sacrificed blood of the precious Lamb of God offers redemption, freedom, and power. He knows power released in believers comes from the blood that has washed over them. Passover is about Jesus, and the last thing our enemy wants is for that message to be celebrated from generation to generation without end. He fights hard for this message never to be heard, believed, and practiced.

We are not attacking the historical leaders of the church in any way. We are merely convinced that a true understanding of the Feasts of the Lord, and specifically Passover, gives Christians an opportunity to experience Jesus in a way they may not have previously known. God tells us in His holy Word that blessings come to those who gain understanding. "Blessed are those who find wisdom, those who gain understanding, for she is more profitable than silver and yields better returns than gold" (Proverbs 3:13–14). "The fear of the LORD is the beginning of wisdom, and knowledge of the Holy One is understanding" (Proverbs 9:10).

The more we seek to gain insight on what is printed in God's holy Word, including understanding of His appointed times, the bigger and greater our God will become. As our knowledge increases, so too will our amazement of our Great God. For the more we know about Him, the more we will understand Him. We should want to watch the entire dress rehearsal unfold before our eyes so our eager expectation of the final performance becomes that much greater. Passover, the first act, set the stage for the remaining six. As the curtain draws to a close, rest assured there is much more to come.

## PERSONAL APPLICATION

The four phrases spoken during Passover, which detail what God said He would do for the Israelites, are exactly what Christ does for us. When we accept Jesus, He says to us, "I will bring you out of the pit of despair. I will free you from the bonds of slavery and oppression. My arms were outstretched on a cross so I could redeem you. I have taken you unto Myself and I have called you Mine."

Write your name in the blanks. Complete each of the first three statements and answer the last.

_____, I have brought you out of the pit of:

_____, I have freed you from:

_____, I have redeemed you from:

_____, do you understand I have taken you as My own?

# seven

Have you ever "come back" to the Lord after living in a land of captivity? What did you do to show your appreciation to Him, to show your faith in the redeeming power of His love?

# CHAPTER 3

# Feast of Unleavened Bread

You will not abandon me to the [grave], nor
will you let your faithful one see decay.

PSALM 16:10

I n the desert of Egypt, a multitude of God-fearing people sat, hastily eating their meal, waiting for the Lord to act. They had faithfully spread the life-saving, sacrificial blood on their homes and were sitting on the edges of their seats, waiting. The day was Nisan 15, the day after Passover. Pharaoh had commanded Moses to take the Israelites and leave to go worship the one they called Lord. As the Egyptians were burying their firstborn, the Israelites gathered all they could carry and set out on a journey that would forever shape the nation of Israel. Read Exodus 12:31–39 and list any details you find important in the story of the Israelites' exodus and the references to bread.

# seven

With the dough they brought from Egypt, they baked cakes of unleavened bread. The dough was without yeast because they had been driven out of Egypt and did not have time to prepare food for themselves. (Exodus 12:39)

Unleavened bread—bread made without yeast, also called the "bread of affliction"—is the centerpiece of the second of the Lord's Feasts, the Feast of Unleavened Bread. Bread that had no time to rise, no time to ferment, and was eaten in haste became what God used to symbolize sanctification.

On the fifteenth day of that month the LORD's Feast of Unleavened Bread begins; for seven days you must eat bread made without yeast. On the first day hold a sacred assembly and do no regular work. For seven days present an offering made to the LORD. And on the seventh day hold a sacred assembly and do no regular work." (Leviticus 23:6–8)

Before the appointed feasts were given to Moses, God had already "set apart" the first two. The Feast of Passover and the Feast of Unleavened Bread walk hand in hand. They are the only feasts instituted before the Israelites were brought out of the land of Egypt, before they were freed from oppression and slavery. Read Exodus 12:7–11. What three things mentioned in verse 8 were the Israelites to eat on the night of Passover?

Unleavened bread was one of three specific foods to be eaten on the night of the Passover in Egypt, and it becomes the focal point for days following the Passover celebration. Look at verses 14–16 and list God's instructions detailed in Exodus 12.

In verse 15, the phrase "without yeast" is derived from the Hebrew word *hametz*, which means "sour." Hametz is "leaven," or any food containing grain and water in which the yeast has been allowed to ferment, causing the food to rise. *Matzah*, the Hebrew word for unleavened bread, is bread that has not been allowed to ferment, sour, and then rise.

God's hand moved quickly through Egypt the night of Passover. He knew time would be of the essence, and that meant the Israelites would not be able to prepare food for their journey. There would be no time for the bread to rise before the people would need to tuck in their cloaks and leave town. Not only did the Israelites consume matzah during their Passover meal, but they also carried it with them as they fled their captors. God in His love for His people was providing for their needs before the needs ever arose.

Exodus 12:17 is where we see this unsoured, distinctive bread given a name and a special place in the worship of the Lord, their Deliverer. Write out verse 17.

In this particular verse we find the second feast given its name: the Feast of Unleavened Bread, or the *Hag Hamatzot* in Hebrew. Why does God say to celebrate, observe, and pay careful attention to this feast? Because on this day the Israelites were brought out of slavery into a land of freedom ("On this very day . . . I brought your divisions out of Egypt"). God was saying this to His people before He ever stretched out His redemptive hand and saved them. Passover had not yet occurred, and yet here we find God explaining to His chosen what He was going to do for them.

## DAYS OF CELEBRATION

God wanted the Feast of Unleavened Bread to impact His people, so He instructed them to celebrate it for a specific number of days. We see direction given first in verse 15 and then again in Exodus 12:18–20. Read the verses printed below. Circle the numbers given and underline any reference to bread.

> "In the first month you are to eat bread made without yeast, from the evening of the fourteenth day until the evening of the twenty-first day. For seven days no yeast is to be found in your houses. And anyone, whether foreigner or native-born, who eats anything with yeast in it must be cut off from the community of Israel. Eat nothing made with yeast. Wherever you live, you must eat unleavened bread." (Exodus 12:18–20)

# seven

Read and write out Exodus 23:14-15.

At the beginning of this lesson we looked at Scripture from the book of Leviticus, which gives a little more detail than what is written in Exodus. Below, mark in some distinguishing way any words or phrases similar to ones found in Exodus 23:14-15.

"'On the fifteenth day of that month the Lord's Feast of Unleavened Bread begins; for seven days you must eat bread made without yeast. On the first day hold a sacred assembly and do no regular work. For seven days present an offering made to the Lord by fire. And on the seventh day hold a sacred assembly and do no regular work.'" (Leviticus 23:6-8)

Over the course of seven days, the people were to hold two sacred assemblies and were not to participate in any activity that would be considered work. For the entire week they were not to consume any foods containing grain except for matzah. In the first month of each year, seven days are set apart to commemorate the sanctifying work of the Lord. Through the remembrance of

Passover, one focuses on the justifying work of the Lamb, and through the Feast of Unleavened Bread, one focuses on the act of being made pure, sacred, and set apart—sanctified.

## RID THE LEAVEN

Remove the yeast! This direct and to-the-point command is spoken by Moses when giving instructions to the people before the night of Passover in Egypt. He speaks of it twice to make sure they do not miss the seriousness of what is being said. Let's go back to the first time God gives instructions for this feast, in Exodus 12:14–20. What was to happen to those who consumed anything with yeast in it during this seven-day period?

The Hebrew word for "cut off" is *kārat*, meaning "expelled." If yeast was found or consumed, those members of the community were to be cast out and expelled from the rest of the people. The degree of consequences connected to disobeying God's command for this feast indicates how intent God is about removing leaven (sin) for the purposes of worship.

Biblically, leaven is the souring agent that represents sin. Sin is what makes us unholy before the Lord. Purity or sanctification is what is needed to enter into the presence of our Holy God. This is the message at the heart of the Feast of Unleavened Bread: remove the hametz and come before the Lord as a people set apart for the holy purposes of God.

## JESUS IN UNLEAVENED BREAD

*Lechem Elohim* (Bread of God) in Unleavened Bread

Then Jesus declared, "I am the bread of life." (John 6:35)

Jesus was not only the sacrificial Passover Lamb; He was also the "Bread of Affliction" who sanctified us all. Our Savior is the fulfillment of being the "sin-free" unleavened bread. Bethlehem, a town whose name means "House of Bread," birthed Jesus, the Bread of Life. We have seen symbolism throughout the life of Jesus, and now we will see how it follows Him to His death and burial in the grave. Turn to the book of Hebrews and see how the author describes our Savior. Read Hebrews 4:14–15 and fill in the blanks.

"Therefore, since we have a great high _____
who has ascended into heaven, _____
the Son of God, let us hold firmly to the faith we
profess. For we do not have a high priest who is unable
to _____ with our weaknesses, but we
have one who has been tempted in every way, just as
we are—yet he did not _____"

Write out Hebrews 7:26 in the given space.

What words of the prophet Isaiah did Peter use to describe Jesus in his first letter written to believers (1 Peter 2:22)?

Which of these words describe attributes of Jesus as Paul spoke of Him in 2 Corinthians 5:21?

☐ Perfect     ☐ Gracious

☐ Sinless     ☐ Merciful

Though He was tempted, He remained holy. Though He was tried, He never defiled Himself. Jesus, our Messiah, was pure and sinless in every way. With every step He trod and every word He spoke, Jesus was and still is the living matzah—unleavened and without sin.

## seven

## BURIED BREAD

Nisan 15, the day the Egyptians buried their firstborn, is the same day God buried His Firstborn. One of the most cherished prophecies concerning Messiah is found in the book of Isaiah. Read the entire chapter of Isaiah 53 and note anything that may correlate to what we have studied so far.

What does Isaiah 53:9 specifically state about Messiah's burial?

Isaiah is saying He who knew no sin became sin for us and died a criminal's death. A guilty verdict in the days of Christ meant a criminal's death and, therefore, a criminal's burial. Dying as a "criminal," Jesus would have been consigned to be buried in a trench outside the city walls of Jerusalem. His body would have been tossed flippantly into an open grave with countless others, left to decay and rot with the rest of the convicted felons of His day. Yet when our Savior was removed from the tree on which He hung, He was not thrown haphazardly into that criminal's grave. According to Luke 23:50–53, what happened to Jesus' body following His death?

Read the following passage from Matthew 27:57–60, and circle all words and phrases that support the fact that our Lord was indeed assigned a rich man's grave, just as Isaiah prophesied.

As evening approached, there came a rich man from Arimathea, named Joseph, who had himself become a disciple of Jesus. Going to Pilate, he asked for Jesus' body, and Pilate ordered that it be given to him. Joseph took the body, wrapped it in a clean linen cloth, and placed it in his own new tomb that he had cut out of the rock.

Joseph of Arimathea, a man of wealthy means, had most likely purchased this tomb for his own and his family members' burial in the future. Notice that the tomb was new; it had never been used, never been defiled by a decaying body. Our Savior, the perfect sacrifice, who took upon Himself the weight of our sins, was indeed honored with the burial custom of a rich man. He was assigned a grave with the wicked yet was buried among the rich. Even in His burial, the Father esteemed His Son, making a clear proclamation of His innocence.

## NO DECAY OF THE BREAD

God's proclamation regarding Messiah did not stop at the door of the tomb. God had no intention of letting His Son see decay. Read the prophetic words of King David: "You will not abandon me to the [grave], nor will you let your faithful one see decay" (Psalm 16:10).

Who is the Holy One David is referring to?

What do you think "You will not abandon me to the [grave]" means in regard to the Holy One?

What will the Holy One not see?

David, King of Israel, in the bloodline of Jesus, was not speaking of himself but was foretelling of the One who was to follow him, the One who would reign as King forever. God did not allow the body of Jesus to be kept in the grave to see decay. The body of the Son would not return to dust but would rise up from among the dead and live again. Recall, matzah is bread that has not been allowed to ferment or sour; therefore the decaying process never begins. Neither did the decaying of Christ, the living matzah, ever begin. Although His body was buried, it would never deteriorate but would stay as whole as it was the day He died.

> On the first day of the week, very early in the morning, the women took the spices they had prepared and went to the tomb. They found the stone rolled away from the tomb, but when they entered, they did not find the body of the Lord Jesus. While they were wondering about this, suddenly two men in clothes that gleamed like lightning stood beside them. In their fright the women bowed down with their faces to the ground, but the men said to them, "Why do you look for the living among the dead? He is not here, he has risen! Remember how he told you, while he was still with you in Galilee: 'The Son of Man must be delivered over to the hands of sinners, be crucified and on the third day be raised again.' Then they remembered his words." (Luke 24:1–8)

The earthly body Jesus inhabited while His presence graced this world never experienced what inevitably follows death—decay. The Father protected His Son by preventing this natural process to occur. God was making a statement through this action: "My Perfect Son, blameless in all His ways, became sin for you and died a criminal's death. But the curse of death and destruction has no hold on Him. My Son truly is the Unleavened Bread."

## OBSERVANCE

In the days of Jesus, Passover and the Feast of Unleavened Bread were no longer celebrated as two separate feasts. They had been combined into one weeklong celebration and are still celebrated that way today. The Feast of Unleavened Bread was one of three yearly occasions when Hebrew men were required to present themselves to the Lord in worship.

> "Three times a year you are to celebrate a festival to me. Celebrate the [Feast] of Unleavened Bread; for seven days eat bread made without yeast, as I command you. Do this at the appointed time in the month of Aviv, for in that month you came out of Egypt. . . . Three times a year all the men are to appear before the Sovereign LORD." (Exodus 23:14–15, 17)

Three times from the beginning of the harvest season until the end of the harvest season, the men were to appear before the Lord. The first of those times was the Feast of Unleavened Bread. God wanted them to remember that, like the matzah, they too had been set apart, sanctified.

Scriptures tell us Jesus celebrated this annual observance not only as a man but also as a child. We know He was in Jerusalem preparing for the feast and celebrating the Passover meal when He was arrested, tried, and executed. But years before His death, we find Jesus in His Father's house, presenting Himself before the Lord.

Look up Luke 2:41–43 and fill in the blanks.

Every year Jesus' parents went to _____ for the [Feast] of the Passover. When he was _____ years old, they went up to the [feast], according to the _____. After the [feast] was over, while his parents were returning home, the boy Jesus _____ behind in Jerusalem.

Jesus celebrated the feast as a young boy but fulfilled the feast as a man.

## A SIGN

"This observance will be for you like a sign on your hand and a reminder on your forehead that this law of the LORD is to be on your lips. For the LORD brought you out of Egypt with his mighty hand." (Exodus 13:9)

The Hebrew word for "sign" is 'ôt, meaning "mark, token, memorial, symbol, proof; signifies anything which could be shown or confirmed; pertaining to past, present or future." A "reminder," or *zikkārôn*, is "a token act by which something is brought to mind, including visual objects."

In the days prior to Messiah's death on the cross, the people of God used unleavened bread as a symbol of the Lord's deliverance. The yeast-free matzah was a visible token to them, proof that the mighty hand of God removed them from the depths of their depravity and gave them a new life. The matzah was not to be something of the past but, as God instructed, a symbol that needed to be shown then, now, and forevermore.

Jesus, the true Matzah, celebrated Passover on the night before His death. He gave His followers a new sign confirming who He was and instituting a new way of remembering what He has done for those who believe.

Write out Luke 22:19 below.

In Paul's letter to the church in Corinth, he mentions the words and directives of Christ. Below is 1 Corinthians 11:23–26. Circle any words found both here and in Luke 22:19.

For I received from the Lord what I also passed on to you: The Lord Jesus, on the night he was betrayed, took bread, and when he had given thanks, he broke it and said, "This is my body, which is for you; do this in remembrance of me." In the same way, after supper he took the cup, saying, "This cup is the new covenant in my blood; do this, whenever you drink it, in remembrance of me." For whenever you eat this bread and drink this cup, you proclaim the Lord's death until he comes. (1 Corinthians 11:23–26)

Jesus was saying, "Do this in remembrance of Me. This bread is to be for you a sign of My body that was sacrificed. May this bread, broken and then eaten, always bring to mind the significance of My redeeming love and the new life you have gained." Just as God gave the Israelites a sign to remember their deliverance, Jesus gave all who call Him Savior a sign to remember their deliverance as well.

# seven

"Today you are leaving." This was God's message to the Israelites, and it is God's message to us. Many of us have chosen to apply the blood to our "doorframes," but have we chosen to "leave"? Have you ever left something and followed after God? Or maybe He is calling you to leave now. Explain below.

The Jewish community worked diligently to remove all leaven from their homes in preparation for the feast. Leaven represents sin. Has God ever asked you to remove leaven in your life?

"This observance will be for you like a sign on your hand and a reminder on your forehead that this law of the LORD is to be on your lips. For the LORD brought you out of Egypt with his mighty hand" (Exodus 13:9). A sign is something that evokes a memory from us. Do you have signs (maybe a token or journal) that remind you of God's greatness in your life?

# CHAPTER 4

# Feast of Firstfruits

HE IS TO WAVE THE SHEAF BEFORE THE LORD SO IT
WILL BE ACCEPTED ON YOUR BEHALF.

LEVITICUS 23:11

For years the Israelites had wandered through the vast, dry landscape of the Sinai Peninsula. They had moved from place to place, from sand to more sand, with manna and quail as their only source of food. Forty years after their great exodus, the time had come to enter the Promised Land. Only after entering into a land flowing with milk and honey would they have a harvest to reap, a harvest with which to praise God and offer up its firstfruits. It was now time for the third Feast of the Lord to be celebrated, the Feast of Firstfruits.

The LORD said to Moses, "Speak to the Israelites and say to them: 'When you enter the land I am going to give you and you reap its harvest, bring to the priest a sheaf of the first grain you harvest. He is to wave the sheaf before the LORD so it will be accepted on your behalf; the priest is to wave it on the day after the Sabbath. On the day you wave the sheaf, you must sacrifice as a burnt offering to the LORD a lamb a year old without defect, together with its grain offering of two-tenths of an ephah of finest flour mixed with oil—an offering presented to the LORD by fire, a pleasing aroma—and its drink offering of a quarter of a hin of wine. You must not eat any bread, or roasted or new grain, until the very day you bring this offering to your God. This is to be a lasting ordinance for the generations to come, wherever you live.'" (Leviticus 23:9–14)

According to the Scripture above, on what day was the priest to wave the sheaf of grain?

The one-day feast designated to celebrate the firstfruits of the barley harvest occurs the day after the Passover Sabbath. Faithful Jewish followers observed Passover and the Feast of Unleavened Bread; then the day following that week's Sabbath, the priest would wave the grain offering to the Lord in celebration of the provision of God's hand. The first three feasts occur one right after the other, all within the same week and all within the first month.

Look again at the Scripture above. What were the people to bring the priest?

The word *sheaf* comes from the Hebrew word *omer*, meaning "measure." The first grains to be harvested every year were the barley. The harvesters threshed the grain from the fields, beat it to remove the chaff, and then ground it into flour. It was an omer, or a measure, of this flour that became the firstfruits offering made to the Lord. The Hebrew word for "first" used in the verse above is the word *resiyt* (from the Hebrew word *rōʾš*), meaning "head; first as to place, time, order, rank; first of its kind." We have seen *rōʾš* before in our study of Passover when God informed His people, "This month is to be for you the first month" (Exodus 12:2). Once again the Lord is being specific in regards to "firsts." The Great I AM wanted to make sure the people remembered He was the one who had blessed them with their harvests. He was saying, "Remember Me, honor Me, bring to Me the very first of what you cut from the fields."

Another Hebrew word in the midst of these Scriptures offers us further insight. Take a look at Leviticus 23:11. Check which word or phrase tells why the priest was instructed to wave the sheaf of grain before the Lord.

for show _____ forgiveness _____ to

be accepted _____

**Accepted** (*Rason*): "To be pleased with; favor, grace, kindness; denotes the reaction of a superior to an inferior; used to signify God's favor toward a petitioner."

The first sheaf of harvested grain was brought before the Lord and waved before His all-seeing eyes as a thanksgiving offering. This omer of barley was a representation of the entire harvest. Its purpose was to serve as a pledge that the remaining harvest would be seen as acceptable before God.

We find firstfruits mentioned again in Deuteronomy. This book penned by Moses focuses on summarizing the laws given to the Israelites so future generations might understand and obey. The following Scripture passage provides a description of a special firstfruits grain offering given by the Israelites after their first year in the Promised Land.

Read through the passage. Circle any words that have to do with acknowledging the Lord (our actions) for what He has done or given us, and underline all references to what God has done (His actions).

When you have entered the land the LORD your God is giving you as an inheritance and have taken possession of it and settled in it, take some of the firstfruits of all that you produce from the soil of the land the LORD your God is giving you and put them in a basket. Then go to the place the LORD your God will choose as a dwelling for his Name and say to the priest in office at the time, "I declare today to the LORD your God that I have come to the land the LORD swore to our ancestors to give us." The priest shall take the basket from your hands and set it down in front of the altar of the Lord your God.

Then you shall declare before the LORD your God: "My father was a wandering Aramean, and he went down into Egypt with a few people and lived there and became a great nation, powerful and numerous. But the Egyptians mistreated us and made us suffer, subjecting us to hard labor. Then we cried out to the LORD, the God of our ancestors, and the LORD heard our voice and saw our misery, toil and oppression. So the LORD brought us out of Egypt with a mighty hand and an outstretched arm, with great terror and with miraculous signs and wonders. He brought us to this place and gave us this land, a land flowing with milk and honey; and now I bring the firstfruits of the soil that you, LORD, have given me."

Place the basket before the LORD your God and bow down before him. Then you and the Levites and the foreigners among you shall rejoice in all the good things the LORD your God has given to you and your household. (Deuteronomy 26:1–11)

"Bring the best of the firstfruits of your soil to the house of the LORD your God," Moses directs the people in Exodus 34:26. But why? David gives us the answer in Psalm 24:1: "The earth is the LORD's, and everything in it, the world, and all who live in it."

Everything belongs to the Lord, every animal from the land, every fruit from the trees, every grain from the fields. What God desired from His people was a concentrated mindfulness that it was He who redeemed them, set them apart, and brought them into a land of freedom. The Lord had given them everything they needed for life and godliness. This feast was to be a special time of recognizing the Lord for the bountiful land He had given to them. It was a thanksgiving offering made at the beginning of each harvest season as a visual reminder of thanking the One from whom all blessings flow.

## JESUS IN FIRSTFRUITS

*Hamoshia l'chol Adam* (Savior of All Men) in Firstfruits

To affirm Jesus' fulfillment of the Feast of Firstfruits, we must pay careful attention to the timing of the days to know what was occurring outside of the grave.

Look up Luke 18:31–33 and Matthew 28:1, 5–7. Using the space below, summarize what Jesus said about Himself and what Mary saw when she visited the tomb. Keep special focus on the days mentioned.

On Friday afternoon Jesus died as the Passover Lamb. On Saturday, which was both the Sabbath and the Feast of Unleavened Bread, His body lay in a tomb covered in spices and grave clothes. While death had taken hold of Christ, the hold would not last. On Sunday, the day after Passover Sabbath, the Feast of Firstfruits was taking place at the temple. The priest was in the courtyard with his arms held high before the Lord, offering up the firstfruits of Israel's harvest. On that same Sunday, death lost its grip on Jesus and He was raised from the dead.

One, two, three. In the year of Christ's death, we see the three feasts celebrated in consecutive order on consecutive days (Nisan 14, 15, and 16). Only the Almighty God could have planned these events with such perfect timing.

> On the first day of the week, very early in the morning, the women took the spices they had prepared and went to the tomb. . . . They did not find the body of the Lord Jesus. . . . The men said to them . . . "Remember how he told you . . . 'The Son of Man must be delivered over to the hands of sinners, be crucified and on the third day be raised again.'" (Luke 24:1–7)

We can imagine that, as the burial linens fell off His body, the arms of the Son raised high in praise and thanksgiving to the Father. Christ sacrificed Himself as an offering to the Lord, as an atonement for all who would believe in Him. By doing this, Jesus became the firstfruits of the rest of the harvest, a whole harvest sanctified. A harvest full of those who believe in Him as Lord and Savior.

In his letter to the church in Corinth, Paul spoke of Christ's resurrection and what that means for those who believe in Him. Record below Paul's words found in 1 Corinthians 15:20–23.

Jesus' resurrection was proof that God accepted the sacrifice, that the offering was enough to cover the debt. With the assurance of the resurrection we know our sins were covered and wiped clean. "As far as the east is from the west, so far has he removed our transgressions from us" (Psalm 103:12).

In the book of John, we come to the account of Jesus raising Lazarus from the dead. Before Jesus acts, He explains. Pick up the story beginning in John 11:17 and read through verse 26. What was Jesus' "I am" statement to Martha?

What did Jesus say would happen when a believer in Him dies?

After Jesus rose from the grave, He returned to the earth for 40 days. During that time, He appeared before and spoke with many people, proving His resurrection and preparing them for the days when He would no longer be with them. Jesus then ascended into heaven and took His rightful position at the right hand of God until the time comes for the rest of the harvest (believers) to be called home.

> For the Lord himself will come down from heaven, with a loud command, with the voice of the archangel and with the trumpet call of God, and the dead in Christ will rise first. After that, we who are still alive will be caught up together with them in the clouds to meet the Lord in the air. And so we will be with the Lord forever. (1 Thessalonians 4:16–17)

Our enemy wants nothing more than to see death rule in the world. It is his ultimate weapon against humankind. But resurrection defeats it. Resurrection makes no compromise with death but instead completely overthrows it. Jesus is the Resurrection, the firstfruits of many, and those who have put their faith in Him will not feel the sting of death but will be alive with Him in eternity. Christ is the Firstfruit of the Great Harvest.

In the Feast of Firstfruits we once again see God confirming His salvation plan to us. Through the resurrection of Christ, we have a guarantee of the promises of God. We can stand strong in our faith, knowing our belief has been placed correctly into the hands of the Almighty One.

## OBSERVANCE

While the traditional ceremonial practices surrounding the
Feast of Firstfruits no longer occur today, one important ritual
still takes place: counting the omer, or measure of time from the
third feast to the fourth feast. In essence, the Feast of Firstfruits
acts as a "time marker."

What specific instructions are given to Moses in Leviticus
23:15 with regard to the Feast of Firstfruits and the counting
of days?

Moses is told to count off seven full weeks, 49 days, seven
sets of seven. Seven, the number representing completion or
perfection, is the number the Lord wanted used to count off
the days from the Feast of Firstfruits to the time of the summer
harvest. The arrival and celebration of the summer harvest is
marked by the celebration of the Feast of Weeks. The Feast of
Weeks is solely connected to the celebration of the firstfruit. The
latter relies on the former; the harvest is completely dependent
on the firstfruits.

Before we focus our sights on the fourth feast, let us
remember that Jesus fulfilled all three spring feasts, each with
different meanings and symbolisms. With Passover, the Lamb of

God offered Himself as a living sacrifice for all who have sinned. Like the matzah in the Feast of Unleavened Bread, Jesus, our "sin-free" bread, was buried. Yet His body did not decay. And just as the Feast of Firstfruits celebrates the beginning of the spring harvest, so too is Christ the beginning of God's harvest. His resurrection clearly states that Jesus is the firstfruit of all who will be resurrected. As believers in Christ Jesus we can rest in the assurance of what the first three feasts of the Lord mean for us:

- We have been ransomed, redeemed, and justified.
- We have been declared holy, set apart, and dedicated.
- We will be raised up and delivered into eternal life.

# CHAPTER 5

# Feast of Weeks

"I WILL ASK THE FATHER, AND HE WILL GIVE YOU
ANOTHER HELPER, THAT HE MAY BE WITH YOU
FOREVER; THAT IS THE SPIRIT OF TRUTH.
JOHN 14:16–17 (NASB)

Counting the omer had commenced—49 days; seven sevens counted off from the Feast of Firstfruits. It was the beginning of the summer harvest and the last of the spring feasts; the Feast of Weeks was upon the nation. Seven weeks after presenting themselves to the Lord at the Feast of Unleavened Bread, the men of Israel gathered at the temple once again to bring sacred offerings to the Lord.

"Three times a year you are to celebrate a festival to me. . . .
Celebrate the [Feast] of Harvest with the firstfruits of the crops
you sow in your field. . . . Three times a year all the men are
to appear before the Sovereign Lord." (Exodus 23:14, 16–17)

# seven

Read through the instructions given for the Feast of Weeks (Feast of Harvest) in Leviticus 23:15–21. What was to be counted from the day after the Sabbath?

How many days were to be counted off?

Here we see two different numbers, seven and 50; seven weeks and 50 days. The significance of both numbers cannot be overlooked, for they are directly tied to the Hebrew and Greek names given to the feast. Seven weeks were to be counted in preparation for the final spring feast, *Shavuot*. The Hebrew name for the feast has its roots in the action of the counting, for Shavuot literally means "weeks." But we find the modern-day name in the Greek language: "Pentecost," which literally means "fiftieth." Shavuot, the Feast of Weeks, was celebrated after the counting of weeks, on the fiftieth day, the day of Pentecost.

In Leviticus we see this feast is "dateless," for a specific date is not given; days and weeks had to be counted to arrive at the appointed time. The counting of days is an act of remembrance. To observe Shavuot one would have to remember and observe Passover. The celebration of the bountiful harvests of the land depended on the people's remembering they had been redeemed, set free, and delivered. Just as each feast is connected and builds upon the feast that precedes it, ultimately they all rest upon the foundation of Passover. As this day of celebration arrives it looks a bit different from the previous feasts. Going back to Leviticus 23:16–21, list out the specific instructions given for the Feast of Weeks.

The ceremonial practices of this feast are similar to the previous feast in bringing the firstfruits to the Lord. The firstfruits of the barley harvest had already been offered to God; now it was time to present the firstfruits of the wheat harvest. There is one small difference, however, between the bread offerings of the third and fourth feasts. Look back at Leviticus 23:17. What was to be mixed with the flour to make the bread offering?

# seven

The bread made for the celebration of the Feast of Firstfruits was unleavened; it contained no yeast (remember, this feast occurred during the seven-day period of the Feast of Unleavened Bread). In contrast, the bread made specifically for the celebration of the Feast of Weeks was to be made with yeast. During the morning sacrifice at the third hour (nine o'clock), the priest would wave the two loaves of bread before the altar of the Lord, and then, instead of being burned as a sacrifice, they were to be given to the priest. "The priest is to wave the two lambs before the LORD as a wave offering, together with the bread of the firstfruits. They are a sacred offering to the LORD for the priest" (Leviticus 23:20).

The Lord had been given His share, and now it was time for the people to recognize the needs of others and give to them. Since the priests who served in the temple were not allowed to work outside the temple, all provisions to sustain them came from the sacrifices and offerings brought by those they represented. With this feast, God may have been reminding the people that He would use what they brought Him to bless others. Blessings and freewill offerings were key elements to the celebration of Shavuot.

Write out Deuteronomy 16:10.

The Feast of Weeks was a celebration of the bountifulness God had provided the people. They were to offer before the Lord what came from the abundance of their crops and from their own free will. It was an offering with no specific amount, no set limit, no boundaries or restrictions. A gift of the heart to their Savior.

## JESUS IN FEAST OF WEEKS

*Ben Ha-Elohim* (Son of God) in Feast of Weeks

From the day of firstfruits, the day Jesus rose from the grave, faithful followers marked their calendars, eagerly anticipating the final spring feast. From day one up through day 40, Jesus appeared to His followers, teaching and discipling them as He prepared them for the One who was to come next. "On one occasion, while he was eating with them, he gave them this command: 'Do not leave Jerusalem, but wait for the gift my Father promised, which you have heard me speak about'" (Acts 1:4).

At the Passover meal Jesus spoke with His disciples about the gift the Father had promised. Read Jesus' words recorded in John 14:16, 26 and 16:7.

Who is the Father going to send to His followers?

What two names does Jesus give to the One who will come in His name?

The words of Jesus speak to a prophecy of old. Isaiah prophesied of One who was to come after the Redeemer and be a covenant of God's love to His people, setting them apart as His. Read Isaiah 59:21. What did the Lord say would be His covenant, and what would that "covenant" do?

Jesus told His followers He would be leaving, but there would be a Helper to follow Him. One who would stay with them forever, who would remind them of His words and keep His truth forever on their lips. This Helper would strengthen them, empower them, and move them to be witnesses for Messiah to the whole world.

> In my former book, Theophilus, I wrote about all that Jesus began to do and to teach until the day he was taken up to heaven, after giving instructions through the Holy Spirit to the apostles he had chosen. . . . He appeared to them over a period of forty days. . . . On one occasion, while he was eating with them, he gave them this command: "Do not leave Jerusalem, but wait for the gift my Father promised, which you have heard me speak about. For John baptized with water, but in a few days you will be baptized with the Holy Spirit. . . . You will receive power when the Holy Spirit comes

on you; and you will be my witnesses in Jerusalem, and in all Judea and Samaria, and to the ends of the earth." After he said this, he was taken up before their very eyes, and a cloud hid him from their sight. . . . Then the apostles returned to Jerusalem from the hill called the Mount of Olives, a Sabbath day's walk from the city. . . . When the day of Pentecost came, they were all together in one place. (Acts 1:1–5, 8–9, 12; 2:1)

Forty days into the counting of the omer, Jesus ascended to heaven. But not before He gave His disciples specific instructions not to leave Jerusalem but to stay in the city. Given that the Feast of Weeks was only a few days away and each of the men would need to present themselves at the temple once again, it's unlikely anyone questioned this directive. Write out word for word what Acts 2:1 says.

Ten days after Jesus ascended to heaven came the day of Shavuot, or Pentecost. There, in the Holy City, something was about to happen, a gift that would change believers' lives forever. The temple courts were bursting with Jews who had traveled from as far away as Rome, Mesopotamia, and Asia. They had gathered to hear the traditional Scripture readings from Ezekiel and Habakkuk, prophetic words spoken from God as a message to His people. Turn

to Ezekiel 1:4–5, 13, and 20. What prophetic words would have been spoken as the morning temple service commenced?

Every God-fearing Jew and follower of the Lord who gathered at the temple listened to the reading of this prophecy.

The followers of Jesus were gathered in a home, waiting as He had commanded them to. Read Acts 2:1–4, making notes of any similarities between what occurred in Acts and the prophecy of Ezekiel.

According to Acts 2:5–6 what happened next?

"When they heard this sound." It was the third hour, the time of the morning sacrifice. At the same moment the priest presented the offering, the crowds of people worshiping in the temple courts heard the sound of a violent wind. The Spirit of the Lord came down from heaven to abide with the followers of Christ, fulfilling God's covenant promise. The Spirit moved as if by fire to rest on the tongues of those designated to speak the Word of the Lord, and all the people present heard their own languages spoken.

Luke, the author of Acts, says the people were amazed, bewildered, and perplexed as they listened to Peter and the others declaring the wonders of God in their own languages (Acts 2:7–12). Peter addressed the crowd, refuting accusations that they were drunk. "These people are not drunk as you suppose. It's only nine in the morning! [the third hour]" (v. 15). He then quoted the prophet Joel:

> "'In the last days,' God says, 'I will pour out my Spirit on all people. Your sons and daughters will prophesy, your young men will see visions, your old men will dream dreams. Even on my servants, both men and women, I will pour out my Spirit in those days and they will prophesy. . . . And everyone who calls on the name of the Lord will be saved.'" (Acts 2:17–18, 21)

Peter continued his discourse by pointing to the account of Jesus' death and resurrection, quoting prophecy from David and the fulfillment of those spoken words by the One they had crucified. Roughly three thousand people became believers on the day of Pentecost and received the "gift of the Holy Spirit" (Acts 2:38).

The first celebration of Shavuot, following Christ's death and resurrection, resulted in God's giving His people a gift from His heart, the gift of the Holy Spirit. Thousands heard God's word and were cut to the heart, choosing to freely give themselves to the Lord. They offered the best thing they could: their hearts and their faith. And out of His abundant love, God gave them His Spirit in return.

## TWO LOAVES

On the day of Pentecost, while the two loaves of bread made from the newest wheat harvest were being waved at the temple, two "loaves" of people were being filled with the Spirit.

> And how is it that we each hear them in our own language to which we were born? Parthians and Medes and Elamites, and residents of Mesopotamia, Judea and Cappadocia, Pontus and Asia, Phrygia and Pamphylia, Egypt and the districts of Libya around Cyrene, and visitors from Rome, both Jews and proselytes. (Acts 2:8–10 NASB)

Luke says both Jews and proselytes heard the words of Peter and were cut to the heart. The word *proselyte* comes from the Greek *proserchomai*, meaning "to come, to approach." Proselytes were considered strangers or foreigners who came from one people to another. They dwelled among the Jews and embraced their religion. They were not of Jewish descent, yet they believed in the Lord and had spiritually come near to Him. The offering of two loaves is distinct to Shavuot, and this is the only feast where one finds this directive specifically written (Leviticus 23:17). The two loaves represent two distinct groups of people, Jew and Gentile. God solidified the acceptance of the proselytes when the Holy Spirit moved in their hearts and fulfilled the Feast of Weeks. The gift of the Counselor (Helper) was made available to all who believed, both Jew and Gentile (proselytes).

In God's Word we see "two" as a consistent theme connected to a witness, or witnessing. Two witnesses were required by Jewish law for a testimony to be acceptable. Deuteronomy 19:15 says, "One witness is not enough to convict anyone accused of any crime or offense they may have committed. A matter must be established by the testimony of two or three witnesses." God demanded two people give witness or speak on a matter; only then would it be accepted as truth.

When Jesus sent the disciples out to preach, heal the sick, and cast out demons, how did He send them? (Mark 6:7)

How many witnesses does Paul tell Timothy are necessary to handle disputes within the church? (1 Timothy 5:19)

According to Revelation 11:3, how many witnesses will speak out against the Antichrist?

# seven

With the sacrifice of Jesus complete, the two loaves represent the united body of believers, both Jews and Gentiles. The message of Christ was never meant to be limited to one people; it was meant for all. Through the work on the cross, Jews and Gentiles have been united in a new covenant.

> But now in Christ Jesus you who once were far away have been brought near by the blood of Christ. For he himself is our peace, who has made the two groups one and has destroyed the barrier, the dividing wall of hostility, by setting aside in his flesh the law with its commands and regulations. His purpose was to create in himself one new humanity out of the two, thus making peace. (Ephesians 2:13–15)

The Feast of Weeks was fulfilled on the day of Pentecost when the Spirit of the Lord descended upon believers. The origination of the church age began when the Holy Spirit filled the room where the disciples were waiting. In that moment God made a statement: The church, or God's body of believers, would be marked by a new sign, the sign of the Spirit, and that sign didn't differentiate between Jew and proselyte. The only qualification was the acceptance of Jesus as Messiah. The Feast of Weeks established one church and one body; it is a beautiful picture of the whole body of Messiah: Jew and Gentile.

## OBSERVANCE

The celebration of Shavuot still occurs today as observing Jews count seven sets of seven from the time of Firstfruits to the Feast of Weeks. The religious ceremony has changed due to the destruction of the temple, and a shift has occurred in its focus. Shavuot and the law of Moses became connected with one another through the Talmud (the central text for Jewish rabbis). After this the focus changed from an agricultural festival to one centered on celebrating the giving of the Torah.

In the third month, about 50 days after leaving Egypt, God met with Moses on Mount Sinai and gave the Torah, the written law, to the Jews as instructions for their daily lives.

> On the first day of the third month after the Israelites left Egypt—on that very day—they came to the Desert of Sinai. . . . On the morning of the third day there was thunder and lightning, with a thick cloud over the mountain, and a very loud trumpet blast. Everyone in the camp trembled. . . . Mount Sinai was covered with smoke, because the LORD descended on it in fire. (Exodus 19:1, 16, 18)

With the new focus, Shavuot now extends throughout the night as observers study and discuss the Torah. Scriptures describing the glory of the Lord from Ezekiel and Habakkuk are still read, and the book of Ruth is recounted.

Whether one was a believer in the early church or is a follower of Christ Jesus in the modern church, one thing is certain: Pentecost is still occurring. The indwelling of the Holy Spirit continues to manifest in all who proclaim Jesus as Lord. The Feast of Weeks, celebrated ten days after Jesus ascended to the Father, has extended throughout the generations to us today.

## PERSONAL APPLICATION

James 1:18 says, "He chose to give us birth through the word of truth, that we might be a kind of firstfruits of all he created." Just as the early Christians were a sign that a great number of people would come to believe in Christ Jesus, we as individual faith-followers can also be a kind of firstfruit for the Lord. Maybe you are the first faith-follower in your family or the only Christian in your place of work. Think about the opportunities in your life. How might God use you as the first of many? Is there an open door for you to become the firstfruit where God has planted you?

Knowing Jesus is our firstfruit, what assurance does that give you when you think of your heavenly home?

In the Feast of Weeks, God gave the people an opportunity to give a freewill offering. Why is this important? Have you ever given God or someone else a freewill offering? If so, how did it make you feel?

## FOCUS

Israel's four springtime feasts were fulfilled during the first coming of Jesus. As our focus shifts to the three remaining feasts in the fall, one must understand these feasts are yet to be fulfilled. While they have been celebrated for generations (dress rehearsal), the redemptive fulfillment (real act) is still a future date known only to God. It is our belief the fall feasts will be fulfilled in order just as the spring feasts were, one building upon the next. We know from biblical prophecy that these feasts will be fulfilled through Christ. Therefore it is of great importance that we keep our focus on Him and Him alone. We are commanded to search Scripture, and Scripture testifies of prophecies yet to be fulfilled. Jesus Himself repeatedly reminded His disciples to watch for His future arrival, and Paul said we are to be informed, not ignorant, so the day does not surprise us.

A complete understanding of the feasts aids us in looking at the book of Revelation and future prophecy, as the two are intricately connected. Although much of future prophecy remains a mystery, we understand that one day we will reign with our heavenly Father. But the details of how and when are not always clear. When our search becomes about specific signs and not about Jesus, we are focusing on the wrong thing. No matter the many different beliefs held by people on the details, we can agree on this: Jesus is coming back for His followers, and one day we will reign with God. Jesus is our focus, the central theme; He is all that matters.

## seven

We believe the Word of God contains both literal and symbolic meanings. Different views are held on the literal and symbolic interpretation of future prophecy; we encourage you to approach Scripture with an open mind, always testing beliefs against the written Word of God.

# CHAPTER 6

# Feast of Trumpets

For the Lord himself will come down from heaven, with a loud command, with the voice of the archangel and with the trumpet call.

1 THESSALONIANS 4:16

Autumn has arrived, and harvesting continues in the grain fields. Stalks are threshed and kernels ground into flour. The storehouses fill up with grains reserved for the winter months. Six months have gone by since the beginning of the Jewish religious new year, and the seventh month, Tishri, is upon the nation. As its numerical significance implies, it is a month representing completion and perfection. All three remaining Feasts of the Lord are found within Tishri. These are the fall feasts, and no time will be wasted; the first day of the month begins with the Feast of Trumpets, the fifth of the seven feasts.

The Lord said to Moses, "Say to the Israelites: 'On the first day of the seventh month you are to have a day of sabbath rest, a sacred assembly commemorated with trumpet blasts. Do no regular work, but present a food offering to the LORD.'" (Leviticus 23:23–25)

"'On the first day of the seventh month hold a sacred assembly and do no regular work. It is a day for you to sound the trumpets.'" (Numbers 29:1)

According to the Scriptures, what are the three specific things the people were to do on this day?

The Feast of Trumpets lasts for just one day, but it is a unique day. This is a sabbath day, when the people rested from what demanded their time and energy to focus on bringing offerings before the Lord. The Day of Blowing, or *Yom Teruah*, was a time to fill the air with the sound of the trumpets, a tone so distinct and rich it demanded the attention of all who heard it. This feast coincided with the monthly burnt offerings that were presented to the Lord on the first day of every month, as it is the only feast celebrated on the first day of the month. Bringing young bulls, lambs, grains, and bread was a practice to which the people were already accustomed, but making the day a sabbath and blowing the trumpets made it unique. The instructions for the feast are few and the focus specific. The day was to be memorialized, and the central theme was the trumpet.

## TRUMPETS

Two types of trumpets have been used by the Israelites throughout their history: the silver trumpet and the *shofar*. Both are distinct in appearance and sound, and both are used for various purposes. First we will focus on the silver trumpet, or the *hatzotzerah*, as it is known in Hebrew.

One year after being freed from the hand of Egypt, the Israelites were in the desert celebrating Passover. The Lord's presence had descended among the people and He could be visibly seen in the form of a cloud by day and fire by night. The Tent of Meeting, God's resting place, had been constructed, and now it was time for the next task. According to Numbers 10:1–2, what were the Israelites to make?

What were their purposes?

The people were to take a precious metal, hammer it, beat it, and shape it into something that could produce a magnificent sound. The metal is shaped into a long, straight tube with one end slightly expanded for the mouth and the opposite end flared for sound. The horn was used to summon the people together, as well as to let them know it was time to move.

The shofar is made from the horn of a ram (*shofar* in Hebrew means "ram's horn trumpet"). Naturally curved in shape, it is accepted among the Hebrew people as a reminder of the Lord's providing a ram, caught in the thicket, as a substitute for the sacrifice of Abraham's son, Isaac. While the Bible doesn't specifically designate which of the trumpets was to be used for the Feast of Trumpets festival, the Jewish rabbis traditionally designated the shofar.

A few verses later, in Numbers 10, we see the Lord giving additional purposes for the sounding of the trumpets. In the Scripture below, circle the other reasons given for blowing these special horns.

> "When you go into battle in your own land against an enemy who is oppressing you, sound a blast on the trumpets. Then you will be remembered by the LORD your God and rescued from your enemies. Also at your times of rejoicing—your appointed [feasts] and New Moon feasts—you are to sound the trumpets over your burnt offerings and fellowship offerings, and they will be a memorial for you before your God. I am the LORD your God." (Numbers 10:9–10)

The Lord expressed the three different times He desired the trumpets to be sounded:

*1. When you assemble the community.*
"Blow the trumpet in Zion, declare a holy fast, call a sacred assembly" (Joel 2:15).

"Sound the trumpet throughout the land! Cry aloud and say: "Gather together!"" (Jeremiah 4:5).

*2. When you go into battle.*

"Sound the trumpet in Gibeah, the horn in Ramah. Raise the battle cry in Beth Aven; lead on, Benjamin" (Hosea 5:8).

"For I have heard the sound of the trumpet; I have heard the battle cry" (Jeremiah 4:19).

*3. When you rejoice in My appointed times.*

"Make music to the LORD . . . with trumpets and the blast of the ram's horn" (Psalm 98:5–6).

"Sound the ram's horn at the New Moon, and when the moon is full, on the day of our festival" (Psalm 81:3).

This will be important to remember as we begin to look at the connection between Jesus and this feast. The significance and symbolism of the trumpet and its uses are the keys to unlocking the mystery of that connection's fulfillment.

## JESUS IN FEAST OF TRUMPETS

*Hu Haba* (The Coming One) in Feasts of Trumpets

"Then will appear the sign of the Son of Man in heaven. And then all the peoples of the earth will mourn when they see the Son of Man coming on the clouds of heaven, with power and great glory. And he will send his angels with a loud trumpet call, and they will gather his elect from the four winds, from one end of the heavens to the other." (Matthew 24:30–31)

What happens when the trumpet is sounded?

The Son of Man will appear with great power and glory, and His trumpet will sound, signaling the gathering of all who have put their faith in Him. The Day of Blowing will take on a new meaning as the trumpet sounds in the sky. During the celebration of the Feast of Trumpets, the shofar is blown one hundred times with a pattern of blasts which repeats 11 times (totaling 99 blasts). The final, one hundredth blast is known as the "Last Trump." With that in mind, look at 1 Corinthians 15:51–52 and fill in the blanks below.

"Listen, I tell you a mystery: We will not all sleep, but we will all be changed—in a flash, in the twinkling of an eye, at the last _____.
For the trumpet will _____,
the dead will be raised imperishable, and we will be
_____."

Paul references the words of Christ in his first letter to the church of Thessalonica. He gives greater detail of this event to ensure a deeper level of understanding for those who are waiting for the coming of the Lord.

First Thessalonians 4:13–17 is printed for you below. Circle the words or phrases that correlate to any of the feasts we have studied so far, and underline what happens at the sound of the trumpet.

Brothers and sisters, we do not want you to be uniformed about those who sleep in death, so that you do not grieve like the rest of mankind, who have no hope. For we believe that Jesus died and rose again, and so we believe that God will bring with Jesus those who have fallen asleep in him.

According to the Lord's word, we tell you that we who are still alive, who are left until the coming of the Lord, will certainly not precede those who have fallen asleep. For the Lord himself will come down from heaven, with a loud command, with the voice of the archangel and with the trumpet call of God, and the dead in Christ will rise first. After that, we who are still alive and are left will be caught up together with them in the clouds to meet the Lord in the air. And so we will be with the Lord forever.

The undeniable tone of God's trumpet will sound, and its blasts will fill the air above all the earth. Every ear will hear the blowing of the trumpet, but for those who know Him, it will have a special meaning. When the trumpet of the Lord, the last trump, is sounded, it will be time to gather the assembly. Time to bring together those whom Christ calls His own, both those who have "fallen asleep" and those who still have breath. The assembling and gathering of the masses is what believers today refer to as the "rapture of the church." Jesus will fulfill the Feast of Trumpets when He raptures the church at the sound of the trumpet.

The word *rapture* means "caught up," and while Scripture does not give specifics as to when the trumpet will sound, one thing has been revealed to us: the trumpet that will call all believers home will be blown by none other than the Lord. Turn to Zechariah 9:14 to look at the prophetic words surrounding the trumpet blast of God. What does the Word say will happen when the Lord appears?

The Sovereign Lord will sound the trumpet. Not angels, not heavenly bodies, not those on earth, but the Lord God Almighty Himself. The trumpet call of God, which Paul prophesied in 1 Thessalonians, is exactly what Zechariah is referring to here. There are only two occasions in Scripture where the Lord blows the trumpet. The first was on Mt. Sinai:

> On the morning of the third day, there was thunder, lightning and a thick cloud on the mountain. Then a shofar blast sounded so loudly that all the people in the camp trembled. Moshe brought the people out of the camp to meet God;

they stood at the base of the mountain. Mount Sinai was enveloped in smoke, because Adonai descended onto it in fire. . . . As the sound of the shofar grew louder and louder, Moshe spoke; and God answered him with a voice. (Exodus 19:16–19 Complete Jewish Bible)

The first trumpet blast by God took place three months after the Israelites' exodus from Egypt. The chosen people of God assembled at the base of the mountain and watched as God descended upon the mountain. When God blows the second trumpet, His chosen people will be gathered once more and will ascend to Him in the heavens.

## PURPOSES FOR THE TRUMPET CALL

Look back a few pages at the purposes for which God said the trumpet was to be used (Numbers 10:9–10). What were the three times designated for sounding the trumpet?

We have already examined the fulfillment of the first purpose of the sounding of the trumpets: to assemble the community. Now we will see how the remaining two purposes are fulfilled and also look at a fourth.

## THE BATTLE CRY

"When you go into battle in your own land against an enemy who is oppressing you, sound a blast on the trumpets. Then you will be remembered by the LORD your God and rescued from your enemies" (Numbers 10:9).

While they were still wandering in the desert, before a battle was ever laid before them, God said to the Israelites, "When you go into battle, sound the trumpets." From the book of Joshua on through the Old Testament, we can see God's people doing just that. Was it a warning of danger and destruction, or was it a call to get ready, to be prepared? The answer is both. The sound of the trumpets was just as much a warning to their enemies as it was a call to action by those who would be doing the fighting. The battle of Jericho recorded in the book of Joshua tells us specifically that the shofar was blown as the men went into battle against their enemies. Read Joshua 6:1–5. Write down the specifics you feel are most interesting.

# seven

For six days the priests blew their trumpets as they walked around the city walls with the warriors. The entire town of Jericho heard the shofar blasts and trembled with fear at the warning call—a call that peril and destruction were headed their way. A call to the men marching to prepare themselves for the battle that was about to take place. Then on the seventh day the shofars blew and the walls came tumbling down.

In Ezekiel's prophetic warnings to the nation of Israel (33:1–3), he says this:

> "Speak to your people and say to them: 'When I bring the sword against a land . . . and [the watchman] sees the sword coming against the land and blows the trumpet to warn the people, then if anyone hears the trumpet but does heed the warning and the sword comes and takes their life, their blood will be on his own head.'"

To whom was this warning directed?

God uses the trumpet blasts to warn of ensuing battles for both His enemies and His people. When they heard the trumpet, they were to prepare themselves—either for ensuing danger or to stand up and fight. When God sounds the trumpet on the day of the rapture, it will also be a warning call, a warning to those living on earth that the biggest and most important battle of history will soon commence. It will also serve as a warning call for the armies of heaven to ready themselves for the anticipated campaign against the enemy of the Lord, Satan. Thankfully the outcome of the battle has already been determined, and one can stand firm knowing that the blast of God's trumpets will usher in that victory.

## REJOICE AT THE APPOINTED TIME

"My Father's house has many rooms. . . . I am going there to prepare a place for you. . . . I will come back and take you to be with me that you also may be where I am" (John 14:2–3)

These are the words of Jesus as He begins to comfort His disciples after telling of His betrayal and Peter's future denial of Him: "I will come and take you to be with Me." This has been the hope of the church since it flowed from the lips of our Savior. One day He will return, and when He does He will take us with Him. The trumpet will sound and the rejoicing will begin as our hope in being with Him will be fulfilled.

Why will there be rejoicing at the sound of the trumpet? Read 1 Thessalonians 4:17 to answer the question.

After this I looked, and there before me was a great multitude that no one could count, from every nation, tribe, people and language, standing before the throne and before the Lamb. (Revelation 7:9)

People from every nation and tribe will rejoice at the trumpet sound, knowing it is God's signal calling us to our eternal home. John spoke of this home in Revelation when he said, "Never again will they hunger; never again will they thirst. . . . [The Lamb] will be their shepherd. . . .God will wipe away every tear from their eyes" (Revelation 7:16–17). The Bible tells us we will be overjoyed when the glory of Jesus is revealed, and no one will be able to take away our joy. We will truly be able to live the exhortation of Paul when he said, "Rejoice in the Lord always. I will say it again: Rejoice!" (Philippians 4:4).

## CORONATION OF A KING

While God stated His purposes for sounding the trumpets, the Israelites incorporated the trumpets into another very important event: the crowning of a king. King David's instructions for the coronation of his son Solomon were "Blow the trumpet and shout, 'Long live King Solomon!'" (1 Kings 1:34). After the prophet Elisha anointed Jehu king over the Lord's people, his fellow officers spread their coats on the ground beneath Jehu's feet, blew the trumpets, and shouted for their new king (2 Kings 9:13). So too will the trumpets sound for the King of the Jews to usher in His reign.

Jeremiah foretold of Messiah as King when he said, "The days are coming, declares the LORD, when I will raise up for David a righteous Branch, a King who will reign wisely" (Jeremiah 23:5). At the birth of Jesus, the magi came from the east in search of the One they said had been born king of the Jews. Upon first meeting Jesus, the disciple Nathanael declared of Him, "Rabbi, you are the Son of God; you are the King of Israel" (John 1:49).

What are the words of Zechariah found in 14:9?

# seven

The Sovereign Lord will sound the trumpet. Think about that for a moment. God, Creator of all the earth, Ruler over all people, will press a trumpet to His lips and blow a sound unequalled in all history. A sound so commanding, so compelling, so distinct, that every ear around the world will hear the Father announcing the coming reign of His Son. What an amazing moment that will be!

The book of Revelation opens the eyes of its readers to future prophecies yet to be fulfilled. It speaks of many things that will remain a mystery until the day God chooses to reveal them to us. We can, however, be sure of this: the Lamb of God will reign on high. Using your own words, what does Revelation 17:14 say about Jesus?

Read Revelation 19:11–16. What names are given to the rider of the white horse?

God's trumpet call will fulfill four purposes: to

1. Gather the assembly of believers to their Savior.
2. Prepare heaven's armies to wage war against the enemy of God and to warn that enemy of an upcoming battle.
3. Bring about a time of rejoicing in the Lord.
4. Proclaim to the world that a new king, the King of kings and Lord of lords is taking His rightful place on the throne.

While much about future prophecies is uncertain, one thing is without question: our Messiah, Christ Jesus, was prophesied as a king, and while He did not live as one during His first coming, He will reign as one in His second coming.

## OBSERVANCE

The observance of the Feast of Trumpets is recorded only once in Scripture, in the book of Ezra. The Israelites had returned to their homeland from captivity in Babylon and were allowed to rebuild the temple in Jerusalem. Before the temple construction began, Ezra built an altar. Excerpts from Ezra 3:1–6 are printed below. Mark the key or important parts of these verses that correlate to what you have already learned about this feast.

When the seventh month came and the Israelites had settled in their towns, the people assembled together as one in

Jerusalem. . . . After that, they presented the regular burnt offerings, the New Moon sacrifices and the sacrifices for all the appointed sacred [feasts] of the LORD, as well as those brought as freewill offerings to the LORD. On the first day of the seventh month they began to offer burnt offerings to the LORD, though the foundation of the LORD's temple had not yet been laid.

Nehemiah makes reference to this same day in Nehemiah 8:1–2. What happened on this day that corresponds to activities that were to take place during the Feast of Trumpets?

While these are the only references to the Feast of Trumpets occurring throughout Israel's history, we are not to assume the feast did not take place.

## TODAY'S OBSERVANCE

Just as with the other feasts, the Feast of Trumpets centered around activities at the temple. When the temple was destroyed in AD 70, the celebration of the feasts drastically changed. No temple meant sacrifices could not be made and offerings could not be brought before the Lord. To keep the remembrance alive, the Jewish leaders changed the focus. You might recognize the name *Rosh Hashanah*, which in Hebrew means "The Head of the Year." Rosh Hashanah marks the beginning of Israel's civil new year (not to be confused with the religious new year), and after the destruction of the temple the two celebrations became connected. Over time the Feast of Trumpets was overshadowed by the Jewish new year. Rosh Hashanah has become the major celebration, fulfilling dual purposes—celebrating the Day of Blowing and the new year.

The modern-day observance of Rosh Hashanah has a much different feel to it when compared to the historical Feast of Trumpets. Today's observance begins a ten-day period called the "Days of Awe," which begins with Rosh Hashanah and ends on the Day of Atonement (Yom Kippur), the sixth Feast of the Lord. The "Days of Awe" are a time when the Hebrew nation is focused on personal reflection and repentance. The people search deep within their souls with a longing to "make things right" between themselves, God, and others as they concern themselves with God's divine judgment. The traditions of the people are driven from a focus on their future and how they stand with the Lord.

Jewish tradition holds there are three Books of Life open on Rosh Hashanah: one for the righteous, one for the wicked, and one for those in between. Only the Righteous Judge, God, can write an individual's name in one of the three books. If one's name is found among the wicked, it is believed judgment against them is final. If one's name is among the righteous, it is believed God will grant them another prosperous year of life. If a name is listed with those in between, the Days of Awe become extremely important; this time is for the in-betweeners to sincerely repent and turn to God, to then have their names inscribed among the righteous.

While these traditions may seem "embellished," this part of the Rosh Hashanah observance originated from two books in the Old Testament, Exodus and Psalms.

The words of David calling out to God for His favor and deliverance from the wicked are recorded in Psalm 69. What did David ask of the Lord in Psalm 69:28?

In Exodus 32:31–33 we see a conversation between Moses and God regarding sin. In your own words, what was Moses asking of God and what was God's reply to Moses?

A Book of Life is a theme that spans the Old and New Testaments. When John was given a revelation by God, a Book of Life was mentioned again. After reading Revelation 3:5 and 20:12, describe the books mentioned in these two Scriptures.

While the Feast of Trumpets does not look anything like it did in the days of Jesus, the foundation for the traditions and observances still have their roots in God's Word. The one stable constant of this feast throughout history is the key role the shofar plays in the celebration, both past and present. Even today one can hear distinct blasts blown in specific patterns after special benedictions are given by the priests. While the solemn practice of self-reflection and judgment was not mandated by God in His original instructions for the Feast of Trumpets, its scripturally based traditions and customs carry with it a deep meaning. One day a trumpet will sound at His coming, the skies will be filled with His glory, and those whose name the Lord knows will be delivered to Him.

# seven

Trumpets had a variety of uses in biblical days, including rejoicing in God's appointed times. In our world today, believers don't usually blow a trumpet to signal our rejoicing in God, but what are some other ways we can "blow the horn" in celebration of the Lord?

Battle cries have spanned centuries of traditions and cultures, a practice clearly depicted in almost every movie portraying battles and war. While we may not go into physical battle, we certainly experience spiritual battles. In a metaphorical sense, how can you blow your trumpet to sound your battle cry?

"Do not fear, for I am with you; do not be dismayed, for I am your God. I will strengthen you and help you; I will uphold you with my righteous right hand. All who rage against you will surely be ashamed and disgraced; those who oppose you

142

will be as nothing and perish. Though you search for your enemies, you will not find them. Those who wage war against you will be as nothing at all. For I am the LORD your God who takes hold of your right hand and says to you, Do not fear; I will help you. . . . No weapon forged against you will prevail, and you will refute every tongue that accuses you." (Isaiah 41:10–13; 54:17)

What do the words of Isaiah mean to you as you think of going into "battle"?

# CHAPTER 7

# Day of Atonement

ISRAEL WILL BE SAVED BY THE LORD WITH

AN EVERLASTING SALVATION.

ISAIAH 45:17

The trumpets of *Rosh Hashanah* have sounded, and the next Feast of the Lord has arrived. All work ceases once again as the nation joins together in a sacred assembly. This gathering is referred to as the Day of Atonement and arrives nine days after the Feast of Trumpets, on the tenth of Tishri. It is the sixth of the seven feasts and carries with it a reflective tone. It is considered the most solemn day of the year for the Hebrew nation. You may not be familiar with the English name, Day of Atonement, but you may recognize its Hebrew name, *Yom Kippur*. Names reveal so much about a person, a place, or even a thing. Names give identity, and the name of this feast is no different. Its name reveals the meaning as well as the act central to the feast. To fully understand the feast, we must first fully grasp the name.

***Yom***: "day, day of 24 hours."

***Kippur***: derived from the Hebrew word *kaphar*, meaning "to cover; make reconciliation; act of cleansing, forgiving; putting off; being merciful; purging."

**Atonement** (*Kippurim*): "covering; satisfaction or reparation for wrong; the condition which results when one makes amends; to become reconciled; to be 'at one.'"

Yom Kippur, the Day of Atonement, literally means "the Day to Cover." It was a day when the transgressions of Israel would be covered over, the nation would be cleansed of the wrongs committed in the previous year, and amends would be made. A necessary covering was granted by a merciful and Holy God for the sins of His chosen people.

The instructions for this day of covering are given in Leviticus 23:26–32. After reading the Scripture, note in the space below any words or phrases you feel are important regarding this feast.

Sin exists, plain and simple. We all have sinned and fallen short of the glory of God. God is a Holy God who cannot accept unholiness. This means there is a division between man and God, a barrier between holy and sinful. But God's desire has always been to provide His imperfect people with a way to cover their unholiness and restore them into relationship with Himself. This is what the Day of Atonement accomplishes.

We have studied atonement before with Passover, and we know the sacrifice of the lamb represents redemption, a covering over. The difference is, Passover speaks of redemption on an individual level while the Day of Atonement speaks of redemption on a national level. Yom Kippur was and is the most holy day of the year for the Hebrew nation because it is "the day God set apart to restore relationship between Himself and His people."[2]

The restoration of God's relationship with His covenant people can be seen from the beginning of their desert wanderings. The concept of a national covering of sin is evident in the aftermath of events such as the golden calf. Moses, called by God to the top of Mount Sinai, had been gone many days. The people grew impatient waiting for his return and convinced Aaron to help them create a god they could worship and who would lead them. The Lord's anger rose against Israel. He said

---

2 Sam Nadler, *Messiah in the Feasts of Israel* (Charlotte, NC: Word of Messiah Ministries, 2010), 126.

to Moses, "I have seen these people. . . . they are a stiff-necked people. Now leave me alone so that my anger may burn against them and that I may destroy them" (Exodus 32:9–10).

Moses pled with God to spare His people and remember His promises to them. When Moses returned to camp he destroyed the calf, confronted Aaron, and then sent sword-bearing Levites through the camp, killing three thousand people. Pick up the story in Exodus 32:30. What does it say Moses said to the people the next day?

Moses was interceding for Israel. The entire nation had taken part in acts of sin committed against the Lord, and the entire nation needed their relationship restored with their Holy God. Only one man, Moses, was allowed to come face-to-face with God, and it was he who stood before the Almighty, asking forgiveness for those he represented. Moses pleaded for God to cover over the people's sins and let them live. In that moment, Moses was participating in a Day of Atonement; he set the example for what would be asked of the High Priest from that point forward.

> Also on the tenth day of this seventh month there shall be a
> day of atonement: it shall be an holy convocation unto you;

and ye shall afflict your souls, and offer an offering made by fire unto the Lord. (Leviticus 23:27 KJV)

The word afflict found in this text is from the Hebrew word *anah*, meaning "to humble oneself, to bow down." Humility is at the center of this day of covering, for without humility there can be no restoration. One's soul—his or her emotions, mind, and desires—must bow down to the One who atones and saves. As the nation of Israel submitted themselves to the Lord in recognition of their need for Him, they were seeking to be made right with God.

While the instructions to the people for Yom Kippur were few, the ceremony for the priest was intricate and lengthy (Leviticus 16). We are not going to read through the entire chapter, but we encourage you to take some time to acquaint yourself with the details of what God required of the high priest for the Day of Atonement. Presenting yourself before the Lord on behalf of the entire nation was not something to be taken lightly, and the details of the ceremony show the serious nature of what was being asked.

Turn your attention to the verses below so you may understand the importance of this feast to the people of Israel.

The LORD said to Moses: "Tell your brother Aaron that he is not to come whenever he chooses into the Most Holy Place behind the curtain in front of the atonement cover on the ark, or else he will die, for I will appear in the cloud over the atonement cover. . . . Aaron is to offer the bull for his own sin offering to make atonement for himself and his household. . . . He is to take some of the bull's blood and with his finger sprinkle it on the front of the atonement cover; then he shall sprinkle some of it with his finger seven times before the atonement cover. He shall then slaughter the goat for the sin offering for the people and take its blood behind the curtain and do with it as he did with the bull's blood: He shall sprinkle it on the atonement cover and in front of it. In this way he will make atonement for the Most Holy Place because of the uncleanness and rebellion of the Israelites, whatever their sins have been." (Leviticus 16:2–16)

God states three different people for whom Aaron was to make atonement. Who are they?

Where was the blood to be sprinkled?

How many times was Aaron to sprinkle the blood on the cover?

Why was Aaron directed to perform these tasks? What was the purpose behind it all?

The atonement of a nation hung in the balance, and something was needed to keep the scales from tipping. As we learned earlier, Israel needed help being brought back into the righteousness of a Holy God, and the Day of Atonement did just that, for with Atonement came restitution.

Aaron, the priest, was charged with the task of presenting himself before the ark of the covenant in the Most Holy Place of the tabernacle and sprinkling the blood of sacrificed animals onto the cover of the ark where the Lord's presence rested. He was asking for the Lord's covering of sin for himself, his family, and his nation. This was the only day of the year the high priest was allowed to go beyond the curtain that protected the Holy of Holies and stand in the presence of the Most High God. It was both the highest honor as well as the most serious act of reverence you could perform.

# seven

Look up Leviticus 16:34 and record it in the space below.

The Lord had requirements. They were not many, but they were specific and necessary. The requirements for atonement weren't for the benefit of the Lord but for the benefit of the people. They were already sitting in a place of loss, but their merciful God provided a way for them to gain what mattered most: reconciliation with Him.

Unique to this feast is the use of two goats. While several sacrifices were used to atone for the people, goats played a special role. They were always given as a general sin offering. The use of two goats on the Day of Atonement may seem like a minor detail; however, it is one of the most important and central parts of the feast. In Leviticus 16:7–10, we find God's instructions regarding the significance of the two goats. Read the Scripture and use the space below for any words or phrases that stand out to you.

"Then [Aaron] is to take the two goats and present them before the LORD at the entrance to the tent of meeting. He is to cast lots for the two goats—one lot for the LORD and the other for the scapegoat. Aaron shall bring the goat whose lot falls to the Lord and sacrifice it for a sin offering. But the goat chosen by lot as the scapegoat shall be presented alive before the LORD to be used for making atonement by sending it into the wilderness as a scapegoat."

What is the definition of the word *scapegoat* in the dictionary?

Each goat was marked for its intended purpose, either "for the LORD," or "for Azazel," the name given for the scapegoat. Even though two individual animals were used, they were accepted by the Lord as one. For it says in Leviticus 16:5, "He is to take two male goats for a sin offering."

The goat marked "for the LORD" was slaughtered by the high priest as a sin offering for the people (Leviticus 16:15). By sprinkling the blood of the goat upon the atonement cover, "he will make atonement for the Most Holy Place" (v. 16). Now read Leviticus 16:20–22. In what ways is the goat marked "for Azazel" treated differently?

Notice that verse 22 says, "The goat will carry on itself all their sins." Once the blood of the slain goat was sprinkled onto the mercy seat, or the ark of the covenant, the high priest would come out from behind the curtain separating the Most Holy of Holies and lay his hands on the head of the scapegoat. At the same time, he would confess the sins of Israel. This action symbolically transferred the people's sins onto the goat. The scapegoat was then sent away into the desert, where it carried the sins of Israel with it. Both goats served as substitutes for the people; both bore the penalty of sin. While God demanded a covering over of sin with the sprinkling of the blood on the ark of the covenant, He also gave the people a visual reminder of what He does with our sins when we repent—He carries them away.

Of all the specifics surrounding Yom Kippur, the central theme is that a blood sacrifice was necessary to cover over the sins of the people. No one was without sin; everyone needed saving from that sin. But why blood? Because that is where life is found: "For the life of a creature is in the blood, and I have given it to you to make atonement for yourselves on the altar; it is the blood that makes atonement for one's life" (Leviticus 17:11).

Within the blood, through the blood, and because of the blood there is life. Without blood there is only death—true for both animals and humans. The blood of an animal could not save the people, but it acted as a cover over them, hiding all their unrighteousness from the Righteous One.

The act of using blood to cover over wasn't new to the nation of Israel, for it was what God used in their exodus. In faith they covered their homes with blood, which acted as a covering when death passed over the land. Now, here in the desert, the Lord asked them once again to use the sacrificial blood as a covering over not their homes but their nation.

# JESUS IN DAY OF ATONEMENT

*Melekh HaiYehudim* (King of the Jews) in Day of Atonement

Two goats, one offering; one Savior, two purposes—one for the Lord, the other to act as a scapegoat and carry away the sins of the people. Scripture tells us we do not have the means necessary to atone for our own sins. Psalm 49:7–8 says, "No one can redeem the life of another or give to God a ransom for them—the ransom for a life is costly, no payment is ever enough." Jesus is the only one who had the means to accomplish this. He is both God and human, bridging the gap to make an atonement that not only covered over but carried away sin.

We have studied how Jesus, our Lamb of God, fulfilled the necessary sacrifice of Passover. Now we will see how Jesus satisfies the work done by the goats of Yom Kippur. First, the one marked "for the LORD."

Read 1 John 2:2. Given your knowledge of what *atonement* means, what do you believe John is saying about Jesus Christ in this verse?

According to Romans 3:25, how was Jesus presented to the Father?

The Greek word used for atonement in this verse is the word *hilastērion*, meaning "to propitiate; to expiate." To propitiate is to appease; to make favorably inclined. To expiate means one is making amends or reparation for guilt. By acting as our hilastērion, Jesus made amends with the Father on our behalf. His sacrifice absorbed the punishment for sin and causes the Lord to look favorably upon us as our guilt is removed. Just as the blood from the goat was offered before the mercy seat of God to cover the sins of the people, so the blood of Jesus was sprinkled for those He represents. As believers in Christ Jesus, we have incurred divine favor, and through Him we have avoided divine retribution.

Jesus not only satisfied the demand of atonement for sin, but He also served as our scapegoat. He took our sins upon himself and, carrying them away, removed them far from us. After reading 2 Corinthians 5:21 and 1 Peter 2:24, what do we learn about Jesus' role in regard to dealing with our sins?

Now turn the pages of Scripture back to the words of David found in the Psalms. Word for word, write out Psalm 103:12.

As our hilastērion and our azazel, Jesus both appeased and carried, made amends and removed, made us favorably inclined and restored us. Our Savior did not stop at just removing the punishment of our sins; He continued on by carrying our sins into the depths of the sea, to be remembered no more.

## JESUS AND THE FUTURE FULFILLMENT FOR ISRAEL

While Yom Kippur speaks of Jesus' fulfilling the requirements of our atonement, it also speaks prophetically to the nation of Israel—the unbelieving Jewish remnant remaining after the Feast of Trumpets has been fulfilled—regarding repentance, acknowledgment of Messiah, and being brought back into covenant with Him. Much is foretold in Scripture about what will be in the coming days; however, much also remains a mystery. God, in His infinite wisdom, knew that some things needed to be left unsaid to keep the eyes and mind watchful and the heart and soul hopeful.

One thing the Lord chose not to leave unwritten is this: in the last days the world will see nations rise up against Israel, seeking its destruction and demise. This is a day prophesied long ago by God's prophet Zechariah.

> The word of the LORD concerning Israel. The LORD, who stretches out the heavens, who lays the foundations of the earth, and who forms the human spirit within a person, declares: "I am going to make Jerusalem a cup that sends all the surrounding peoples reeling. Judah will be besieged as well as Jerusalem. On that day, when all the nations of the earth are gathered against her, I will make Jerusalem an immovable rock for all the nations. All who try to move it will injure themselves. . . . but Jerusalem will remain intact in her place. . . . On that day I will set out to destroy all the nations that attack Israel." (Zechariah 12:1–9)

Nation upon nation, country after country, people among people will move together with one mission: to destroy Israel. But El Roi, the God who sees, the God who has been waiting and watching, will not let the remnant of Israel fall. He will move His mighty hand and subdue the nations.

Zechariah 14 begins, "A day of the LORD is coming." What does Zechariah 14:3 say the Lord will do?

God did not just reveal this prophetic message to Zechariah; He also showed Joel. What does Joel 3:16 say God will do on the Day of the Lord?

On that day the eyes of Israel's remnant will be opened and their sins atoned. What does this mean? Why are Israel's eyes "shut"?

Turn to Romans 11:7–8 and fill in the blanks below.

"What the people of Israel _____
so earnestly they did not _____.
The elect among them did, but the others were
_____, as it is written: 'God
gave them a spirit of stupor, eyes that could not
_____ and ears that could
not _____, to this very
_____.'"

Israel was given a spirit of stupor and bewilderment, because even though they sought their King earnestly, they rejected Him when He appeared. "He came to that which was his own, but his own did not receive him" (John 1:11). Jesus returned to the Father to wait. "I will go away and return to My place until they acknowledge their guilt and seek My face; in their affliction they will earnestly seek Me" (Hosea 5:15 NASB). Jesus has been waiting, patiently waiting, for the day when His "own" are ready to receive Him as King.

While God's chosen people did not accept His chosen Son, we do know God has not rejected the people, and they have not stumbled beyond recovery (Romans 11:11). We are told that the eyes and ears of the people were shut so the Gentile world would have the privilege of knowing the salvation of Christ. We have gained through their loss. "I do not want you to be ignorant of this mystery, brothers and sisters, so that you may not be conceited: Israel has experienced a hardening in part until the full number of the Gentiles has come in" (Romans 11:25).

The Most High God, who saved Israel first out of the deserts of Egypt, will save them last out of the depths of a fallen world. When salvation to the Gentile world has been fulfilled, God will turn His attention back to Israel. In the last days the remnant of Israel will find themselves in a position of potential annihilation, with the world knocking down their doors, looking to remove their very existence from this earth. While there will seem to be no hope, a great revelation will take place as the people cry out to God to save them from their enemies. Look at Zechariah 12:10. What will happen when the Spirit of the Lord is poured out?

Israel's eyes will be opened and the people will look upon her King and weep. Weep for scorning Him; weep for rejecting Him; weep for piercing Him. The nation will mourn as never before, with a heart full of sorrow and remorse. The people will lament; their souls will be afflicted as they repent and seek forgiveness, and the Lord will forgive them. "On that day a fountain will be opened to the house of David and the inhabitants of Jerusalem, to cleanse them from sin and impurity" (Zechariah 13:1).

On that day the words of Hosea will be fulfilled. Write out word for word the prophetic words found in Hosea 3:4–5.

A spiritual understanding and acknowledgment of the true Messiah will come upon the remnant of Israel, and they will embrace Jesus—His teachings, His miracles, His life, and His identity. Israel will claim Him as Jesus Messiah, the King of kings and Lord of lords. The words in the *Hallel (Psalms 113-118)*, "Blessed is He who comes in the name of the Lord," will be sung with a new meaning of praise and adoration. God will pour out His grace upon the people as He honors His promise of atonement.

Romans 11:26–27 is printed for you below. Circle all words or phrases concerning Israel and underline all words or phrases concerning the Lord.

In this way all Israel will be saved. As it is written: "The deliverer will come from Zion; he will turn godlessness away from Jacob. And this is my covenant with them when I take away their sins."

On Yom Kippur eyes will see, ears will hear, hearts will soften, and all of Israel's remnant will be saved. Jesus will not only atone for the nation but, like the scapegoat, He will remove their sins far from them. Israel will turn to Christ and receive her one and only true King. Because of the grace of God, the Day of Atonement will be a day of full restoration and redemption, gathering the nation back to the Lord.

But Israel will be saved by the LORD with an everlasting salvation; you will never be put to shame or disgraced, to ages everlasting. (Isaiah 45:17)

## OBSERVANCE

The celebration of Yom Kippur underwent adjustments to accommodate for the lack of an appropriate place for offering sacrifices to the Lord. Though the modern observance of Yom Kippur follows more manmade traditions than a biblical observance, Yom Kippur is still considered the holiest day of the Jewish year. Beginning with the celebration of the Feast of Trumpets and continuing for the next nine days, the nation of Israel dedicates itself to the focus of repentance and atonement of their sins. These ten Days of Awe, also known as the High Holy Days, end on the Day of Atonement. On this day, the Jewish people believe the soul of every man will be sealed in either the Book of Life or the Book of Death (or, Book of the Wicked). The day is seen as one's last opportunity to make amends and demonstrate true repentance before the judgment of God is handed down for that year. Israel believes there are three actions one can perform during the Days of Awe that can change the judgment God imparts on Yom Kippur: repentance, prayer, and good deeds. This belief stems from a rabbi who, after the fall of the temple, spoke the words of Hosea, declaring there was another alternative for the atonement of sins that was just as effective.

Look up Hosea 6:6. In your own words, using this Scripture, answer the following question: How did the rabbi use the words of the Lord, spoken to Hosea, to support His rationale of a "new atonement"?

Hosea's words radically changed the observance and traditions of Yom Kippur. Today Yom Kippur celebrations are centered in the synagogues, where five services are performed throughout the day. These services include practices such as prayers, confession, Torah readings, memorial services, and corporate recitation of Scripture. Confessing Jews abstain from daily pleasures such as working, eating and drinking, bathing, sexual activity, and wearing perfumes and lotions, all to dedicate themselves to the solemn traditions of the day. Interestingly, the last service performed on the Day of Atonement ends with the congregation declaring out loud, "Blessed be the Name of the radiance of the Kingship, forever and ever," followed by one long and final blast from the shofar that ends the day's ceremonies.

While Israel's focus is centered on forgiveness, it will never come through the practices of human beings. True forgiveness is found only through the sacrifice of the Lamb.

## PERSONAL APPLICATION

What does it mean to you that Jesus, who is both our sin offering and our scapegoat, not only atones for our sin but completely removes it?

David describes the physical and mental struggles of unconfessed sin this way: "When I kept silent, my bones wasted away through my groaning all day long. For day and night your hand was heavy upon me; my strength was sapped as in the heat of summer" (Psalm 32:3–4). Has there been a time when unconfessed sin caused you anguish before the Lord? Describe your feelings and how you humbly came before God.

Write a prayer of thanksgiving acknowledging God's gift of atonement in your life.

# CHAPTER 8

# Feast of Tabernacles

ARISE, SHINE, FOR YOUR LIGHT HAS COME, AND
THE GLORY OF THE LORD RISES UPON YOU.

ISAIAH 60:1

The hustle and bustle of the excited crowds filled the air with a noise unlike any other time of the year. As the eye scanned the streets of Jerusalem, makeshift huts could be seen in any available space outside the homes and buildings that filled the city. There was much commotion as the preparation for "the Feast" began. What a delightful commotion it was, for the people knew a joyous celebration was about to commence.

The most prominent of Israel's holidays is the Feast of Tabernacles. It is listed by three names in the Bible: *Sukkot*, Feast of Tabernacles, and the Feast of Ingathering. It is the last of God's seven appointed feasts and the third and final pilgrim feast, when the men of Israel were required to present themselves before the Lord. Five days after the Day of Atonement, the nation gathered once again to celebrate God's provisions for them, this time shifting their focus from solemn reflection to jubilant praise. Look at Leviticus 23:33–43. This section of Scripture shows the different elements of Sukkot that are unlike any of the previous feasts. Use the space below to list out as many of the details and fine points of Sukkot as you can.

Verse 42 shines light on where the feast got its name. Exactly what were the people to live in for seven days?

The Hebrew word for "booth" is *sukkot*, meaning "hut, booth, or tabernacle. Basically denoting a temporary abode."

Why did God ask His people to go through the time and trouble to construct something so temporary?

For 40 years after the Israelites were freed from the hands of their Egyptian slave masters, the desert floor was painted with "booths" *(sukkah)*. These temporary residences were not sturdy, stable, or long-lasting, but rather, weak, vulnerable, and easily removed. To an outsider the dotted landscape appeared to be defenseless and easily conquerable. For the Israelites, God was their one and only true security guard. He graciously provided for all their physical needs and also acted as protector during their time in the wilderness. The Feast of Tabernacles—or the Feast of Booths, as it is known by some—is God's great reminder of His provision and protection. The booths constructed for the celebration were meant to symbolize one's dependence on the Lord and served as a visual reminder of all that God had done for the people. Leviticus 23:39 tells us the specific day and month the feast was to occur. But what were the Israelites to do before they celebrated the festival?

The crops of the land, which the people were instructed to gather, did not come from fields of grain but from the vines and trees of the land. The final and biggest harvest of the year was the fruits: olives, grapes, dates, figs, and many more. The feast also celebrated God's continued supply of necessary foods to sustain the Israelites for yet another year.

One unique aspect of this feast is its joyousness, unmatched by any of the other six feasts. The book of Leviticus gives us many of the details surrounding the feast, and Deuteronomy outlines a few more. Read Deuteronomy 16:13–14, and use the space below to write out the first five words of verse 14.

In celebrating the Feast of Weeks, the Israelites were instructed to "rejoice before the LORD." This meant the Lord wanted them to be glad and joyful in worship. They were to take great delight because El Shaddai, the God of Blessings, had given them something exceptionally good: provision and protection. With the harvest season complete and the crops collected, the people could take time to rest, celebrate, and be joyful.

While the sheer joy and great delight associated with the Feast of Tabernacles sets it apart from the other feasts, the number of sacrifices required by the Lord is another important detail that makes Sukkot unique in its celebration. Turn to Numbers 29:12–40. On the first day of the feast, which would be the fifteenth day of the seventh month, the Lord stipulated that three different animals should be used for the burnt offerings. What were they?

The number of bulls that were to be sacrificed decreased by one each day until the number reached seven. On the seventh day of the feast, seven bulls were to be sacrificed as an offering, reflecting completion. Select the total number of bulls to be given as burnt offerings over the course of the seven days.

100 _____ 118 _____ 89 _____

70 _____ 77 _____

# seven

To understand why God specified 70 bulls be given as offerings during Sukkot, we must go back to the story of Noah and his three sons. "Then God blessed Noah and his sons, saying to them, 'Be fruitful and increase in number and fill the earth'" (Genesis 9:1). In Genesis 10 we can read the account of the sons and grandsons of Noah, whose numbers totaled 70. What does Genesis 10:32 say about the clans of Noah's sons?

Write out Deuteronomy 32:8 word for word:

All those who went to Egypt with Jacob—those who were his direct descendants . . . were seventy in all. (Genesis 46:26–27)

The descendants of Jacob numbered seventy in all. (Exodus 1:5)

From the descendants of Noah came 70 nations covering the whole earth, and 70 numbered the direct descendants of Israel. The 70 bulls offered up to the Lord during the Feast of Tabernacles represented the nation of Israel and all the nations of the earth.

While Sukkot extends for seven days, the day after the closing celebration (the eighth day) was also very important to the feast. The eighth day was to be considered a sacred day, a sabbath. *Shemini Atzeret*, the Hebrew name given to that day, was a day of rest. No work was to be done, but offerings were still made by fire. On the first day of the Feast of Tabernacles the Lord said there was to be a "sacred assembly" (Numbers 29:12), and on the eighth day He commanded a "closing assembly" (v. 35). A beginning and an end for the last and final feast.

## JESUS IN FEAST OF TABERNACLES
*Or Ha'Olam* (Light of the World) in Feast of Tabernacles

Two ceremonies are associated with the Feast of Tabernacles. They stand out not only in their importance but also in their fulfillment. They are the Water-Libation ceremony and the Temple-Lighting ceremony. While these ceremonies were not mandated in the written Word of the Lord recorded by Moses, they are accepted as an oral commandment that has been passed down through the generations since the days of Moses.

## THE WATER-LIBATION CEREMONY
## (SACRIFICIAL POURING OF LIQUID)

As the days of summer drew to a close, the nation of Israel was desperately awaiting rain. The months had been hot and the days dry as the people endured what the Jewish Talmud calls the Days of Sun. Now the anticipation for rain runs deep within the heart of every Israelite. The changing of the Days of Sun to the Days of Rain is at the forefront of everyone's prayers, for the people know if there is no winter rain, there will be no crops.

This heightened focus on the need for rain is found in the water libation, or the water-drawing ceremony. Each morning, while the sacrifices were being prepared for the offerings, the high priest, with a golden pitcher in hand, would be accompanied by faithful worshipers as he walked from the temple courts to the Pool of Siloam. This procession would be full of music, dancing, and dramatic celebration as the people followed the priest's every move. Water would be drawn from the pool and carried back to the temple, passing through the Water Gate upon reentry. The priest then proceeded to the stone altar, where he would circle it once, lift the pitcher above his head, and pour the water into a basin on the altar. With the pitcher empty, the trumpets were once again sounded, and music filled the air with praise and worship through the singing of the Hallel. We have seen the recitation of these psalms before with the first feast, Passover. Now we see them again with the seventh feast.

This ritual would continue every morning, but on the seventh day of the feast, the day known as the Great Hosanna (Hoshanna Rabba), the priest would circle around the altar not once but seven times. The volume of the rejoicing crowds increased with each circle the priest made. Their thankful hearts overflowed like the water that was being poured out on the altar: "Praise the LORD, all you nations; extol him, all you peoples. For great is his love toward us, and the faithfulness of the LORD endures forever. Praise the LORD" (Psalm 117).

The only mention of this feast in relation to the life of Jesus is found in John 7. Read John 7:1–39 and answer the questions on the next page.

Jesus, as a devout Jewish man, was required to present Himself at the temple for the Feast of Tabernacles. Why did He delay His arrival in Jerusalem?

When Jesus arrived at the feast, what did He proceed to do and what happened?

Write word for word what Jesus said on the last and greatest day of the feast (verse 37–38).

Oh, the electric emotion that must have been buzzing through the crowds at the temple that morning! For seven days the people had been watching and following the priest as he ceremoniously poured water over the altar in hopes of God's providing what was needed for another year of crops and sustenance. Suddenly, in walks Jesus and announces to those gathered that they need look no further because it is He who provides water that will never run dry. Jesus proclaimed living water would flow from all who believed in Him. "Let anyone who is thirsty come to me and drink" (John 7:37). Anger stirred deeply among the Pharisees as the people questioned who this Jesus was to claim such prophetic words. The people recognized the words of the prophets when they heard them. They knew Zechariah had a vision about the coming of the Lord, a vision of living water and Sukkot.

> On that day living water will flow out from Jerusalem. . . .
> Then the survivors from all the nations that have attacked
> Jerusalem will go up year after year to worship the King, the
> LORD Almighty, and to celebrate the [Feast] of Tabernacles.
> (Zechariah 14:8, 16)

For Jesus to profess these statements, He in essence was saying, "The One you are looking for is here."

On this last and greatest day of the feast, not only are the words of David sung with the Hallel, but so are the songs of praise found in the writings of Isaiah. Isaiah 12:2–6 is printed for you on the next page. Circle any words or phrases you have seen in relation to any of the feasts. Use the space provided to write your interpretation of what Isaiah's words mean in regard to Sukkot.

Surely God is my salvation; I will trust and not be afraid. The LORD, the LORD himself, is my strength and my defense; he has become my salvation. With joy you will draw water from the wells of salvation. In that day you will say: "Give thanks to the LORD, proclaim his name; make known among the nations what he has done, and proclaim that his name is exalted. Sing to the LORD, for he has done glorious things; let this be known to all the world. Shout aloud and sing for joy, people of Zion, for great is the Holy One of Israel among you."

Sing, give thanks, and make His name known among the nations. With joy draw waters from the wells of Yeshua—salvation—for the Holy One is among you. After singing and shouting these prophetic words of praise and adoration, the audaciousness of Christ's words rang in the ears of the leaders and teachers of Israel who wanted to silence Him so desperately.

# THE TEMPLE-LIGHTING CEREMONY

Spirits ran high and the excitement continued as the joyous festivities of the Feast of Tabernacles extended into the night. It was now time for the Temple-Lighting Ceremony (also known as *Simchat Bet Hasho' ayva*—the "Rejoicing of the House of Water Drawing"); this was a celebration of the earlier water-pouring ceremony.

The moon was full, shining through the crisp air as worshipers flooded into the temple courts. Four massive menorahs reaching 75 feet into the air, were placed in the Court of Women. All night long their immense flames glowed. These giant candelabras burned so brightly that their brilliance was said to illuminate the entire city. An incredible sight this was to behold, whether witnessing it from within the walls of Jerusalem or from a distant hill surrounding the city.

With the candelabras ablaze, the dancing and singing commenced. The Sanhedrin would energetically dance throughout the court with torches burning in their hands as the Levites stood at the top of the 15 stairs leading down to the Court of Women, where the menorahs emanated their radiance. The musicians played while the Levites sang the 15 Psalms of Ascent; each new psalm would come with the descent of a stair until they reached the floor of the court.

These amazing celebrations, in which men, women, and children participated, were repeated every night within the temple walls. Rabbis spoke of this ceremony, the *Simchat Bet Hasho'ayva*, stating, "Anyone who has never seen the rejoicing at the place of [water] drawing has never seen rejoicing in all his days."

One can only imagine the energy that must have filled the people, the temple, and the city as they celebrated their God. The measure of light created by this ceremony was unequaled by any other festival, and the joy of those celebrating was immense. This weeklong, day-and-night celebration was something no one wanted to miss, including Jesus.

We learned how Jesus disrupted the water ceremony by declaring that He was the Living Water; now look at another bold statement Christ made immediately following the Feast of Tabernacles. Read John 8:1–2 and fill in the blanks below.

"At _____ he appeared again in the _____ courts, where all the people gathered around him, and he sat down to _____ them."

On the day of Shemini Atzeret, the day after Sukkot, we find Jesus at the temple, preparing to teach those gathered there for the closing assembly on what was a Sabbath day. What were the first words Jesus spoke according to John 8:12?

Another bold claim passed forth from the lips of Jesus. First He stated He was the Living Water; now He is presenting

Himself as the Light of the World. Oh, how he skin of the Pharisees must have crawled as they listened to Jesus' daring statements! His words needed no explanation; they knew what He was claiming, and they called Him a liar. Why the contemptuous attitude of the Pharisees? By saying He was the Light of the World, Jesus was laying claim to the Old Testament prophecies regarding Messiah.

> A star will come out of Jacob; a scepter will rise out of Israel. (Numbers 24:17)

> The Light of Israel will become a fire, their Holy One a flame. (Isaiah 10:17)

> I, the LORD, have called you in righteousness; I will take hold of your hand. I will keep you and will make you to be a covenant for the people and a light for the Gentiles. . . . I will also make you a light for the Gentiles, that my salvation may reach to the ends of the earth. (Isaiah 42:6; 49:6)

Zechariah, the father of John the Baptist, also spoke of the fulfillment of prophecy. Read Luke 1:67–79. According to the words of God spoken through Zechariah in verse 78, what was coming to the people of Israel?

What did the magi see in the sky in Matthew 2:2?

In Luke 2 we read of a righteous and devout Jew named Simeon, who had been promised he would not die before seeing the Lord's Anointed One. According to Luke 2:32, what did Simeon proclaim upon seeing the baby Jesus and taking Him in his arms?

Isaiah 9:22 says, "The people walking in darkness have seen a great light; on those living in the land of deep darkness a light has dawned." Jesus was saying, "I am the Light of the World; a Light that will reach to the ends of the earth."

## JESUS, THE MILLENNIAL KINGDOM, AND TABERNACLES

Just as with the other fall feasts, the fulfillment of the Feast of Tabernacles has yet to occur. The future holds in its hands the unraveling of mysteries that accompany the final feast. But God in His infinite wisdom does not leave us to wonder about much, for He has supplied us with insight that, if read carefully, causes the mystery to seem not so mysterious after all. From the beginning of creation, it has always been God's desire to "tabernacle," or dwell, with all humankind. Whether it was in the garden of Eden, Solomon's temple, or through the Holy Spirit, His desire has always been to be with those who love and put their faith in Him. That desire is seen once again in Sukkot.

Exodus 23 is where we find God instructing Moses about the three times a year the men of Israel were to present themselves before the Lord. This chapter is not new to us, but pay close attention to the particular wording used in verse 16 as God talks about the final feast. Then read verses 14–17. What name did the Lord give the feast that was to be celebrated after all the crops had been harvested?

The Hebrew word for "ingathering" is *āsiyp*, and the root of that word is *asap*, meaning "to gather, harvest, to be gathered, assembled, collected; to bring together." The Feast of Ingathering was designed to be a time of bringing together those who love the Lord and desire to celebrate Him. It was a feast where the nation would gather the people in assembly to worship, praise, and adore their Lord. The Feast of Ingathering also speaks of a future day when Christ will tabernacle with mankind during

His thousand-year reign in the millennial kingdom (Revelation 20:1-6). Zechariah prophesied about this coming reign when he wrote "Shout and be glad, Daughter Zion. For I am coming, and I will live among you," declares the LORD. "Many nations will be joined with the LORD in that day and will become my people. I will live among you and you will know that the LORD Almighty has sent me to you." (Zechariah 2:10-11)

Write out Ezekiel 37:27–28.

Not only will Jesus make His dwelling among people, but His presence will be like a tabernacle. The *shekinah* glory will once again shine in Zion. In the end it will be as it was in the beginning—the Lord will be their light, their shield, their protection.

> Arise, shine, for your light has come, and the glory of the LORD rises upon you. . . . The LORD rises upon you and his glory appears over you. . . . The sun will no more be your light by day, nor will the brightness of the moon shine on you, for the LORD will be your everlasting light, and your God will be your glory." (Isaiah 60:1–2, 19)

What does Isaiah 4:5–6 say about what will be created on Mount Zion when Messiah makes His tabernacle among men?

In this future time of blessing, the glory of God will be evident, just as His glory was visible during the exodus from Egypt.

For one thousand years Jesus will reign as King, during which time He will not only tabernacle among His people, but He will also act as their tabernacle, as their shelter and sanctuary. There will be great rejoicing, fellowship, praise, and adoration—all the things that accompanied the Feast of Tabernacles during the days of old. The redemptive career of Jesus is almost complete. It is abundantly clear that the seven Feasts of the Lord established from the beginning symbolically orchestrate the plan of complete and full redemption found only in Christ.

The third chapter of Zephaniah is a prophetic message regarding the future of the believing remnant. The promises spoken in the second half of the chapter are rich with grace and mercy. You will find Zephaniah 3:13–20 on the next page. Read through it and use the space that follows for any notes, revelations, or thoughts that make it clear to you that God will have His day of ingathering.

"They will do no wrong; they will tell no lies. A deceitful tongue will not be found in their mouths. They will eat and lie down and no one will make them afraid."

Sing, Daughter Zion; shout aloud, Israel! Be glad and rejoice with all your heart, Daughter Jerusalem! The LORD has taken away your punishment, he has turned back your enemy. The LORD, the King of Israel, is with you; never again will you fear any harm. On that day they will say to Jerusalem, "Do not fear, Zion; do not let your hands hang limp. The LORD your God is with you, the Mighty Warrior who saves. He will take great delight in you; in his love he will no longer rebuke you, but will rejoice over you with singing."

"I will remove from you all who mourn over the loss of your appointed festivals, which is a burden and reproach for you. At that time I will deal with all who oppressed you. I will rescue the lame; I will gather the exiles. I will give them praise and honor in every land where they have suffered shame. At that time I will gather you; at that time I will bring you home. I will give you honor and praise among all the peoples of the earth when I restore your fortunes before your very eyes," says the LORD.

God is saying, "I will gather you. I will bring you home. I will give you honor and praise." Century after century God's people have come under attack, suffered persecution, and been oppressed by those seeking to destroy them. In the end, Jesus, will put the sickle to the fields, burning the wicked as chaff and restoring those who have fought so hard for His name. The King of kings and Lord of lords will tabernacle among His people, and He will "rule from sea to sea and from the River to the ends of the earth" (Psalm 72:8).

The worship and celebration of Jesus in Sukkot will continue in the millennial kingdom. Zechariah 14:16 tells us the remaining nations will "go up year after year to worship the King, the LORD Almighty, and to celebrate the [Feast] of Tabernacles." All God's people—the remnant of Israel and the Gentile believers—will be brought together as one to celebrate the Feast of Tabernacles and declare Jesus as King.

The redemptive work of Christ must be finished before the end will come and the new heaven and new earth will be brought forth. The final piece to the redemptive puzzle will be the great white throne judgment. Read Revelation 20:11–15 and describe this day in your own words.

# seven

The eighth day after the week of the Sukkot celebration, *Shemini Atzeret*, was to be a sacred and holy day. In Leviticus God calls it a "closing assembly." Many believe this is the last step before the establishment of the new heaven and new earth, a closing ceremony involving truth and judgment as the Book of Life is closed for good. God will say His final good-bye to those who neglected to accept Jesus as Messiah, those who failed to acknowledge Him as Savior and King. Those whose names are recorded in the Book of Life will be given the privilege of living eternally in the new heaven and the new earth. God will say good-bye to the millennial kingdom and the earth as we know it. With the farewells comes the end of God's redemptive plan; there is no longer any need for it because the bride of Christ will be fully presented to Him and the marriage will be complete.

> Let us rejoice and be glad and give him glory! For the wedding of the Lamb has come, and his bride has made herself ready. (Revelation 19:7)

> And I heard a loud voice from the throne saying, "Look! God's dwelling place is now among people, and he will dwell with them. They will be his people, and God himself will be with them and be their God." . . . He who was seated on the throne said, "I am making everything new!" . . . He said to me: "It is done. I am the Alpha and the Omega, the Beginning and the End" (Revelation 21:3, 5–6)

## OBSERVANCE

The first Sukkot celebration recorded in Scripture coincides with the completion and dedication of Solomon's temple. For 20 years Solomon oversaw the building of the Lord's temple. After much toil and waiting, the time had come for the presence of the Lord to once again be with the people of Israel. First Kings 8 is where we find the story.

> All the men of Israel came together to King Solomon at the time of the festival in the month of Ethanim, the seventh month. . . . The priests then brought the ark of the Lord's covenant to its place in the inner sanctuary of the temple, the Most Holy Place, and put it beneath the wings of the cherubim. . . .
>
> When the priests withdrew from the Holy Place, the cloud filled the temple of the Lord. And the priests could not perform their service because of the cloud, for the glory of the Lord filled his temple. (1 Kings 8:2, 6, 10–11)

Second Chronicles 7:1–3 tells of this same account but uses a few different words. According to these verses, what was described as filling the temple?

God's presence filled the temple, His shekinah glory so thick and tangible even the priests had to cease all normal activity. Solomon proceeded to offer up prayers of dedication to the Lord and blessings upon those gathered around, and then all of Israel took part in the feast. After reading through 1 Kings 8:62–66 and 2 Chronicles 7:4–10, use the space below to comment on what the dedication and celebration of the temple looked like.

What a magnificent sight that must have been as the physical manifestation of God's presence filled the newly constructed temple! Not only were the temple courts bursting with joyous celebration, but the entire city of Jerusalem was likely alive with unspeakable joy and satisfied worshipers as God was now "tabernacling" among them once again.

As with the original celebration of the Feast of Tabernacles, the observance today continues to focus on the presence of the sukkah, or booth. These temporary dwellings with their thatched roofs, with fruits and vegetables adorning the walls, are constructed in the yards or on the patios of observant

Jews. There is no longer a water-drawing ceremony or a light celebration, but the people still keep the feast alive with their rejoicing at the synagogues.

The "Rejoicing of the Law," or the *Simchat Torah*, has now become the central focus of Sukkot. This practice and focal point has its roots in the days of Moses. Just before his death, Moses wanted to make sure the Israelites remembered and understood God's instructions for their lives. He did not want them to forget what had been taught to them over the years. In the words of Moses below, circle the parts of Scripture that would apply to the nation of Israel rejoicing in the law during the time designated for the Feast of Tabernacles.

> Then Moses commanded them: "At the end of every seven years, in the year for canceling debts, during the Feast of Tabernacles, when all Israel comes to appear before the LORD your God at the place he will choose, you shall read this law before them in their hearing. Assemble the people—men, women and children, and the foreigners living in your towns—so they can listen and learn to fear the LORD your God and follow carefully all the words of this law. Their children, who do not know this law, must hear it and learn to fear the LORD your God as long as you live in the land you are crossing the Jordan to possess." (Deuteronomy 31:10–13)

In today's Jewish culture, the reading of the entire Law, the five books of Moses, is read every Sabbath, a little at a time.

# seven

On the day of Simchat Torah, which occurs on the ninth day after the feast begins, the cycle of reading the Pentateuch begins anew as the last chapter of Deuteronomy and the first chapter of Genesis are read aloud from the Torah.

With the exodus of the nation of Israel came a new life, a new beginning, and a new way of doing things. God desired not only to establish Himself among His chosen people, but more important, He desired to reveal Himself to them. Daniel proclaimed to Israel that the God they served reveals deep and hidden things; He reveals mysteries. The appointed Feasts of the Lord are one way God chooses to reveal hidden things to those who care to search within His Word. The feasts hold within themselves mysteries of the Ancient of Days, the Alpha and the Omega, the Beginning and the End. The Lord, in His wisdom, showed us His redemptive plan, not only for Israel but also the world. It is no coincidence that God chose seven feasts, the number for perfection and completion, to represent His redemptive plan for humankind. While we begin with redemption, we have learned we will end with perfection. The feasts have made it clear this was always God's plan: to bring us back into perfection before Him. The way it started in the garden will be the way it will end in heaven: complete, whole, and perfect.

> "So is my word that goes out from my mouth: It will not return to me empty, but will accomplish what I desire and achieve the purpose for which I sent it" (Isaiah 55:11).

## PERSONAL APPLICATION

The Feast of Tabernacles was a joyous occasion. Recall an event or season in your life when you were joyful and rejoicing.

Jesus declared Himself to be the Light of the World and the Living Water. Think of a time when He has either been the light leading your life or the water sustaining you.

Read the verse below, then describe what it means to you knowing you will tabernacle with God.

And I heard a loud voice from the throne saying, "Look! God's dwelling place is now among people, and he will dwell with them. They will be his people, and God himself will be with them and be their God." . . . He who was seated on the throne said, "I am making everything new!" . . . He said to me: "It is done. I am the Alpha and the Omega, the Beginning and the End." (Revelation 21:3, 5–6)

# Bibliography

Biltz, Mark. *The Feasts of the Lord*. Bonney Lake, WA: El Shaddai Ministries, 2008.

Buehler, Dr. Juergen. "The Tower of the Flock." *International Christian Embassy Jerusalem*, November 22, 2012, http://int.icej.org/news/commentary/tower-flock.

Falcon, Rabbi Ted, and David Blatner. *Judaism for Dummies*. Newark, NJ: John Wiley & Sons, 2013.

Howard, Kevin, and Marv Rosenthal. *The Feasts of the Lord*. Nashville, TN: Thomas Nelson, 1997.

Kolatach, Alfred J. *The Jewish Book of Why*. New York: Jonathan David, 1981.

Nadler, Sam. *Messiah in the Feasts of Israel*. Word of Messiah Ministries, 2010.

*Nelson's New Illustrated Bible Dictionary*. Nashville, TN: Thomas Nelson, 1995.

Parsons, John J. "The Jewish Holidays." *Hebrew4Christians.com* (April 2015).

Pierce, Chuck D., and Robert Heidler. "Why Passover?" *ElijahList.com* (April 2015).

Renn, Stephen D. *Expository Dictionary of Bible Words*. Peabody, MA: Hendrickson, 2006.

*Rose Book of Bible Charts, Maps & Time Lines*. Carson, CA: Rose, 2005.

# The Authors

**Tricia Johnson** and **Misty Dollard** are the cofounders of **Ignite Worldwide Ministry**, a teaching ministry designed to make the Bible's theology accessible to everyday believers. Ignite sparks spiritual growth that creates excitement for God and His Word, helping disciples of Jesus "go on to maturity" (Hebrews 6:1).

 **Tricia** has been a Bible teacher and speaker for over ten years in settings of all kinds and sizes, from moms' groups and church Bible studies to retreats, conferences, and more. With an eye for the easily overlooked but important details in God's Word, and with a passion for connecting the Old Testament to practical New Testament living, Tricia teaches today at Willow Creek Community Church. She received her BS in history from the University of Northern Iowa. Tricia and Mike, her husband of twenty years, live in Crystal Lake, Illinois, and are the parents of four children.

*I love taking the discovery of Scripture to a deeper level and teaching others how to pray, speak the Word into their lives, and find God in the little things.* —Tricia

 **Misty** has served for more than ten years as a leader, teacher, and organizer in ministries across the United States. A speaker, author, and editor of Christian articles and books, she seeks to bring God's Word alive in meaning and application for 21st-century believers. Misty also mentors leaders in the body of Christ, helping them cultivate their abilities and character. An outdoors enthusiast, Misty loves hiking and riding motorcycles with Tyler, her husband of ten years. She and Tyler live in Seattle, Washington, with their daughter.

*My passion for serving God comes from a desire to tear down the walls of manmade traditions that keep us from God, and to build warriors for His kingdom.* —Misty

60933154R00114

Made in the USA
Lexington, KY
23 February 2017